The Corralitos

The Corralitos

A Memoir of Ranch Life

Larry Foster

SUNSTONE
PRESS

SANTA FE

Sunstone books may be purchased for educational, business, or sales promotional use.
For information please write: Special Markets Department, Sunstone Press,
P.O. Box 2321, Santa Fe, New Mexico 87504-2321.

Book and cover design › Vicki Ahl
Body typeface › Times New Roman » « Display typeface › Niagara solid
Printed on acid-free paper
∞
eBook 978-1-61139-321-7

Library of Congress Cataloging-in-Publication Data

Foster, Larry, 1945- author.
  The Corralitos : a memoir of ranch life / by Larry Foster.
    pages cm
  ISBN 978-1-63293-026-2 (softcover : alk. paper)
  1. Ranch life--New Mexico. 2. Livestock farms--New Mexico. I. Title.
  F596.F625 2015
  636'.0109789--dc23

                        2014034386

WWW.SUNSTONEPRESS.COM
SUNSTONE PRESS / POST OFFICE BOX 2321 / SANTA FE, NM 87504-2321 /USA
(505) 988-4418 / ORDERS ONLY (800) 243-5644 / FAX (505) 988-1025

Dedicated to Burt Guttman

Preface

The Corralitos, a ranchland covering almost 200,000 acres of high desert, encompasses 300 square miles in southern New Mexico. This memoir is a descriptive narrative of the events and daily routine of tending the cattle and farming the land.

The workload was constant, seven days a week with long hours on horseback and nights spent cutting and baling hay, and the work was dangerous, especially working with the head of 140 cantankerous bulls on a yearly basis. You could never take your eyes off a mean bull. We also grazed 40 head of buffalo and they could be just as ill-tempered and unpredictable and dangerous to handle as the bulls. In addition, we grazed 1600 mother cows and grew 500 acres of alfalfa hay.

The ranch employed six or seven workers and during roundup there could be as many as sixteen. There we up to nine horses in the stable, and they were always shod and ready to ride at any time. There was rarely a slack time, especially during the fall gathering of the herd. It was arduous dirty work, but no one ever complained. The Corralitos saga was one of love, dedication and each new day brought new adventures and memories which will never be forgotten.

1

Lawrence and Howard

I knew Lawrence Daley wasn't a man that a six-year-old boy should be pestering, especially when he was butchering an old cow for cook-house meat and had a razor-sharp knife in one hand. But I could no longer resist the urge to distract his attention and agitate him, so I cautiously circled the big man as he slit the hanging cow carcass front to rear down the belly, disemboweling the cow and spilling the watery paunch, bowels, and viscera onto the concrete floor of the barn. A miasma of thick, pungent odors wafted up from the slick, shiny pile of steaming innards, and I winced at the smell, but still engrossed in the processing, and up to no good, I circled closer and closer to the action. When I couldn't hold back any longer, I shuffled near the big butcher, inching forward and back in short shuffles, just out of arm's reach, and began chiding him.

"Ha, ha, I bet you can't catch me! Ha, ha, ha."

The huge man momentarily looked up from his processing, squinted and eyed me intensely.

"Get out o' here! Go away! I'm cutting ranch meat. Can't you see I'm busy?" he spat back.

"Hee, hee, hee, you're not busy. You can't catch me! Ha, ha," I prodded.

"Get out o' here right now or I'm gonna stick your head in the cow guts," he warned ominously, and then returned his attention to skinning the animal.

I sidled closer, leaning in daringly toward his sphere of control, and chirped at him again,

"Ha, ha, ha!"

But with a quick snatch of his powerful ham-sized hand, he caught my ankle and held it firmly. In an instant he stood up and effortlessly twisted his arm, lifted me, and held me suspended upside-down over the steaming puddle of entrails, intestines, and excreta cut out of the old black cow chained up beside me. Looking up, I saw Lawrence's face glowing, beaming like a cherub with a satisfied smile. Then the muscular arm thrust my head and torso right into the guts below, knocking off my little cowboy hat, pumping and wallowing my upper body in the slather, up and down, like a giant one-armed man churning butter. After a few seconds, with a sucking sound he drew me up out of the belly of the beast and gently plopped me on the concrete. I snapped to my feet a little surprised, hatless, out of breath, with slime dripping down my forehead as I stared once again into his eyes. There was a second of silence. Then Lawrence threw back his head and gave out a raucous crescendo howl, welling from a deep baritone bellow into a shrill, ear-piercing, high-pitched cackle that reverberated off the barns and out-buildings and echoed back from the valley. You could hear his thunderous, chilling laugh for a quarter of a mile. He grinned impishly at me as I stood there, awash in a frothy, stinking mess, and all I could remember was, "Stand your ground, look him in the eye, and don't cry—don't cry!"

Lawrence Daley was an impressive, well-known man from a pioneer ranching family in San Diego County. At age forty he was over six feet tall with a thirty-four inch waist and a muscular, sinuous body. He was agile as a cat, fleet of foot, well coordinated, and would have been any coach's pick for the decathlon. His friends called him "Deer" for his foot-speed, and he was a superb physical specimen. Lawrence was my second cousin, the same age as my father, Pete Foster, and another cousin, Howard Foster, who had grown up together and bonded like brothers. Young Lawrence worked long, tedious hours on the vast land-holdings, ranches, orchards, and farms of the area, and in a thriving construction business owned by his uncle, George, the family patriarch. George, a gruff and straightforward man, was the only person who could, and would, spur Lawrence to attention. Lawrence was terrified of Uncle George. Just the report that George was coming up the road and heading toward the big adobe house was enough to make Lawrence, a huge man, leap out of his stuffed chair and scamper around the house like a mouse, peering out of every window and shaking like a leaf, in fear of his contrary uncle, boss, and benefactor. Lawrence, his wife Bertha, and his son George all cowered many hours at the thought of suddenly having to face the cussed, ill-tempered, crusty old man. But at George's death in 1957, Lawrence and his brother, Donald, inherited more than 50,000 acres of land, as well as a successful road-construction company that worked in and around the San Diego area. It was a growing, booming, bustling San Diego at that time, an era of great prosperity and opportunity; the brothers took control of their acquisitions, hired the best people to work for them, and the business flourished. Likewise, the property values of the ranches appreciated rapidly as the population soared. Daley Corporation was at one time one of the largest freeway-construction companies in California, and the ranches were spread all over San Diego and adjacent counties. Donald oversaw the construction business and Lawrence managed the ranches, and they prospered wherever they went and in whatever they did. Both became wealthy, and the name Daley became synonymous with a growing, vibrant San Diego County.

In addition to being a well-heeled cowman in the southern California ranching industry, Lawrence was also, at times, my babysitter. He and Bertha—a tough, yet tender-hearted woman—helped look after me when my family was relocating after suffering a near bankruptcy from farming in the Imperial Valley. I got jostled around a bit, and sometimes ended up at the Bernardo ranch, waiting to be picked up by Pete or by Sally, my mother, who both worked long hours. Lawrence had various projects underway at all times at five ranches throughout the county, and I loved to ride shotgun with him. He always had some new nifty thing that caught my attention: a four-inch lock-blade knife, or a deer rifle, perhaps a scoped varmint pistol, all neatly displayed in some niche or door panel in the cab of the "Jimmy." He regularly shot deer for ranch meat during the season and was an excellent marksman with any firearm.

On one occasion when we had stopped to open a gate, I started to get out, and he ordered me, "Hold on, stay put!" Unarmed, he opened the door, got out, and slowly stepped toward the gate, bending forward as he went; his gaze glued to the ground, he slowly inched forward, still bending, and then cautiously he lowered his right hand and instantly snatched up a two-foot rattlesnake by the tail, pulling it back toward him. Then he stood and swung the reptile out to his side in small circles, like a cheerleader twirling her pom-pom with just her wrist. The sight of the snake's body became a blur as it whirled, and then Lawrence took a step and gracefully, with a whip stroke, whacked the snake on the top wire of the barbed-wire fence, decapitating the creature with the head, fangs and entrails flying out into the pasture. He casually discarded the writhing carcass at the side of the road, climbed back in the cab, smeared on some chapstick, and squinted over at me with his "See there" stare. He liked to show me he was boss, but I wasn't afraid at all, just impressed with the foolhardy, daredevil act—very impressed.

One hot afternoon riding in the truck, I was bored, not paying attention and bouncing on the seat, when Lawrence told me to sit still so he could drive. But to taunt him I kept banging around on the seat until he blurted out, "What do I have to do to keep your ass still, tie you up?"

"Yeah," I prompted.

He scowled at me, spun the truck in a circle, and made a beeline for the barn. Skidding to a stop, he took me by the arm and pulled me over to the stacked hay, grabbing a rope off a saddle on the way.

"Well if you're so goddamn goosey, let's see you get out of this," he growled. Then he wound the rope around my legs and shoulders, up one side, down the other, back and forth, a hitch here, a cinch there, and in less than a minute he had me hog-tied, lying on my back on the dusty concrete floor, bound up like a horse-hair cocoon, and thinking to myself, "Boy, this will be fun when I get out and give him back his rope."

"I'm getting out of here," I promised, gritting my teeth.

"Watch out for the ants!" He grinned, then jumped into the truck and left.

For a half hour I writhed, grunted, and rolled around on the dirty concrete, huffing, puffing, and jerking back and forth like a Mexican jumping bean, but I managed to get only three fingers free from his rope web, and they were turning numb. I had gotten myself into a tight spot, all balled up on the floor, sweating head to toe, worn out from fighting the heat and the rope. Then suddenly I felt the first ant crawl up my neck, then the second, and I knew then he had won this round. A half an hour longer, hot, swaddled-up, soaking wet, and no longer inching around, I laid there, like a giant, ant-infested spitball, all juiced up, and stuck to the floor. Then I heard boots crackling on the gritty concrete, and Lawrence came into view with a tobacco pipe clenched in his teeth, hesitating, and slowly shaking his head woefully from side to side as he neared, with that "I told you so" look on his face. Slowly he took the pipe out of his mouth, laid his head back and gave out a blasting, bellowing caterwaul, so shrill it hurt my ears. Then, giggling, he untied me. All I suffered were some rope burns, scuffed-up ears, a couple of ant bites, and a slightly bruised ego, which healed quickly when we got in the truck and went back to work.

Often at night I would prod Lawrence into a wrestling match on the living room rug, and always I would end up with whisker burns, struggling as he sat on top of me waiting for Bertha to bring his dinner. In the swimming pool one afternoon I egged him on to a water-fight that ended with my protective aunt, Blanche, rescuing me after he repeatedly dunked my head under water until I was near delirium.

"Lawrence, what the hell are you trying to do, drown that kid?" she bristled as she stormed out the door and confronted him.

"Well, the little bastard won't leave me alone," he bit back.

I loved my aunt's intervention, but I had no plans to curb my small attacks pinching his dominion, or retreating a single inch.

Lawrence's biggest problem was his mouth. He was not an abusive man, never bruised or battered anyone, but his uncontrolled verbal outbursts were punishing and demeaning, especially to the loved ones closest to him. Aunt Bertha and cousin George took the brunt of his bellicose ranting and belittling diatribes. George would avoid Lawrence when he was venting, but Bertha would stand toe to toe with him and defend herself and others with an admirable toughness. Then Lawrence would retreat and go back to work, and Bertha would go into the bathroom, lock the door, run the water, and bawl her head off.

Aunt Bertha was like my second mother, and I wanted to kick Lawrence for the hurtful tongue-lashings he whipped out at Bertha and at George, but kicking him would have been disrespectful and wouldn't have helped anyone. Bertha had most of it right: she stood her ground and looked him in the eye. But then she cried. She sobbed when she should have grabbed a big broom and swatted, whacked, and driven him out the door. He would have understood that, and would have returned with his hat in hand, a more respectful man. At his uncle's death, Lawrence's inheritance produced a man who was generous but unconcerned about the feelings of others. He could be loud, oppressive and stubborn with an unbridled tongue at one moment, then contrite, handing out goodies for retribution the next. He had become like his caustic uncle George, the old man whom Lawrence had dreaded for many years; he had become like a spoiled, mannerless child with no possible guidance or effective direction. Lawrence Daley was to be my boss for the next forty years, and despite all of his failings and shortcomings with people, I loved him. He was family.

If there was an individual who personified post-war agriculture in the southwest United States, that person was Howard Foster. His achievements in cattle feeding, ranching and farming were benchmarks for all his contemporaries and his successors. The digging of the All American canal brought precious water from the mighty Colorado River and turned the inhospitable Mojave Desert sink-hole—one of the driest, lowest, and hottest spots on earth—into a huge bread-basket, a winter wonderland of vegetables, and a cornucopia of crops and cattle. After World War II, there was a population explosion in Southern California, and the Imperial Valley was perfectly situated geographically to provide a constant supply of foodstuffs to the expanding coastal cities—San Diego, Los Angeles, San Francisco—as well as to grow, for the entire nation, winter vegetables that were hard to raise in northern latitudes. Howard spearheaded the creation of large-scale agribusiness in the southwest.

Howard's genius was his curiosity: about how things were put together, how they worked, and how they could they be improved. He loved to take some problematic thing, something that was continually a pain in the neck, and refigure it, fix it, and make it simpler and more efficient. He was forever building better mousetraps. One afternoon while processing cattle in the feed yard he decided that the processing squeeze-chute his crew was using needed to be improved. The iron squeeze-chute's job was to catch and restrain the cattle so the crew could process the animals with vaccination, branding, de-horning, or whatever was necessary. It took four men to operate the manual chute: one to open the door, one to catch the animal's head, one to unlatch the gate, and one or two to lay the chute and the animal on its side. And throughout this process the large animal was shaking, kicking and thrashing, snorting, jumping forward and back, and had become frenzied, angry, and dangerous. When pushing hundreds of animals daily through the cantankerous contraption, there were frequent injuries; cuts, bruises, and broken fingers were commonplace, and the operations caused considerable stress on the livestock. In Howard's mind, this chute was antiquated and needed improvement: to be much heavier and more durable in construction, more power-ful than the large animals it had to restrain, and designed to be operated by fewer people. It needed to be powered hydraulically.

With his shop foreman, Frank, who was a superb welder and machinist, Howard built the chute's prototype using components purchased from local farm-related businesses, parts stores, equipment dealers, and steel and salvage yards. He and Frank worked daily for weeks perfecting and testing the invention at the feed-yard. With the new, efficient chute they developed, the crew was processing cattle faster and more safely than ever before. He patented his squeeze-chute and it wasn't long until word got out about this super chute, one that could be operated by one worker using manually controlled hydraulics similar to those on a front-end loader, with all of the operations being done with two or three fingers on one hand. Soon individuals and businesses became interested in Howard's labor-saving chute, and everyone wanted to buy one as soon as possible. What started out as Howard's effort to solve a big problem for himself ended up solving many people's big problem. Howard couldn't produce the new chutes fast enough, so he franchised the building and sales of the chute to another company, which constructed them under Howard's supervision and to his specifications. Thousands were sold domestically and in Mexico and Canada. It was a phenomenal business success, created and fueled by a persistent, intuitive and inquisitive man. Howard had built a better mousetrap, a much better mousetrap.

The only thing that matched Howard's genius was his mischievous wit. On one hot valley afternoon when the boys were just kids, he and Pete wired shut the door of the outhouse occupied by Howard's father, Orville "Pood" Foster. Pood had been plowing with a team of mules in the field alongside the privy and had stopped to relieve himself. While hc was inside, the boys wired the latch shut, then scampered away giggling and whispering about the great trick they had played on Pood. They loomed just far enough away to watch and hear the commotion coming out of the outhouse, and soon Pood figured out what had happened and began hollering at the boys, "Get me out of here, get me out of here right now or else!"

The boys, knowing Pood's amiable, gentle character, just laughed harder and whispered to themselves, "Or else what?" and erupted into another fit of giggles.

Then Pood threatened, "If you two don't let me out right now, I'm just gonna have to tell Mamma!"

Mamma was Amy, Howard's mother. And all of the fun ended for the boys when her name was mentioned, because with a bony finger wagging in your face, she would deliver, a scathing, scolding, dressing-down, then take away what few privileges you had earned and order you away to clean manure out of the horse stalls. Mamma was no trifling matter, and the boys scurried back to the privy and unwired the latch. Pood emerged sweating, scowling, muttering, and upset that he had lost fifteen minutes of valuable daylight plowing time. The boys pleaded for forgiveness and begged Pood not to tell Mamma, and he just nodded, shrugged it off and went back to his mule team, but Amy found out anyway and vented her anger by assigning the boys additional disagreeable tasks for a week under her hawk-eyed supervision.

Still, the boys never outgrew their passion for pulling pranks on people, and one day, many years later, the object of their tomfoolery was Howard's uncle, Albert "Unc" Caillaud. Unc and his wife, Martha, were retired and, in 1964, were in the first housing development of the city of Rancho Bernardo, land that was originally 6,000 acres of farms and ranch pasture owned by the Daleys. The area lay adjacent to the old Bernardo Ranch headquarters, where my parents and I were living and working at the time. Howard stopped by for a visit and a break in his busy schedule, and took an immediate interest in a small mongrel dog that had wandered into the compound in the morning. The little pooch continually scampered around, lifting his leg and urinating on everything in his erratic path. Howard was fascinated with the uncontrollable cur's ability to pee so abundantly, never missing a tree or tire, then retracing his potty trail and doing it all over again. So he was sure the small, incontinent dog was the perfect accomplice to pull a fast one on old Unc. Of course, Pete had to be involved in the prank, and even I was mustered to drive the truck and abet Howard's impish plot against the unsuspecting Unc.

It was a simple plan of deception: Howard knew that Unc detested two things—vagrants and dogs peeing on his pansies. So Howard raided the clothes closet and dragged out a musty, faded, knee-length old overcoat, and a rumpled rain hat that was stuffed in the pocket; then he donned the ragged coat, lifting the collar up over his neck and pulling the wrinkled, worn-out hat down over his forehead to obscure his eyes and ears, and thus Howard's freeloader disguise was complete. On his way out he grabbed a scratched-up old cane from the garage and hung it on his arm just to add flair to his camouflaged outfit. He had morphed into a bona fide tramp. Then he fashioned a dog leash with a length of old cotton rope and gave the small, thirsty, kinky-haired mutt a big dish of water, which the pooch lapped up eagerly. With the dog snug in Howard's arms, we all headed out in the pick-up to visit Unc.

We arrived at the corner six houses away from Unc's, and Howard hopped out with the dog, he and Pete jabbering last minute instructions, each one egging the other on with smiles and giggling. It was pure kid's stuff, and as Dad and I headed to Unc's house, hunchbacked Howard and the pup were christening the corner fire hydrant, and I thought to myself, "Oh, man, how did Howard ever come up with this one?" We arrived and parked at the curb alongside a pretty path full of flowers leading to the house, and were met at the door by the smiling, amiable Unc and glowing Aunt Martha, both so happy to see us. Unc suggested we sit out in the covered patio overlooking the beautiful, lush flower garden along the path heading to the sidewalk, which was a perfect vantage point, a box seat for the spectacle about to take place. We sat, and Martha poured and delivered hot coffee and offered us donuts, while jocular Dad began chatting about this and that, praising Unc for his beautifully manicured yard, pointing at curious things and asking Unc about them, while the old man answered, his smiling face radiant in response. Then Howard emerged on the sidewalk, hunched over, doddering and poking his cane around in the flowers as if looking for a cigarette butt, with the dog pulling on the makeshift leash, halting every five seconds to lift his leg and spray pee all over Unc's beautiful pansies, here and there, round and round, darting to and fro, smelling and then peeing at will without cessation. Dad, seeing immediately what was unfolding, pursed his lips, grimaced and held back the laughter. Then he pointed at Howard and asked, "Hey, Unc, what's that old man doing out there? That doesn't look very neighborly to me."

Unc slowly arose, his stare glued on Howard and the pup. Then, like a creaky old jack-in-the-box, he sprang out of the chair and landed in a crouch, his bulging eyes blazing, skin stretched back on his face, mouth gaping, and canine teeth flashing like a large, enraged monkey, and he shrieked through the screened porch, "Hey, you! Hey, you! Get that goddamn dog out of my flowers, right now! Get out of here, both of you! Get! Get!"

Unc's angry eyes met Howard's morbid, shadowed stare, and there was an instant of standoff. Then Howard slowly raised his cane, pointed it like an index finger right at Unc's distant nose, and wagged it up and down in solemn warning, while the dog turned small cartwheels up against the rows of plants and peed on everything.

Further enraged, Unc shrilled at him, "I'm coming out there, you son-of-a-bitch, and you better be gone!" Then he mashed open the screen door, socking his fists into the air, huffing and puffing and already out of breath as he emerged, while Howard still wagged the cane. Now the mutt, trying to protect Howard, was yapping and growling at Unc, and I thought to myself, "This will be hilarious if Unc doesn't die!"

Then Aunt Martha chimed in from the porch window, "Albert, you calm down now, and don't go out there. Listen to me, Albert, you stay put!"

Now Dad, Howard, and I realized that this little ruse had gone too far, seeing the old man in a fit of intense anger and turning red with rage. So we started to placate Unc: "It's okay, Unc, it's only Howard! Unc, it's that damn Howard, Unc!" Dad persuading, patting the old warhorse on the back.

"Easy does it, Unc," I chimed in, "It's your crazy nephew, Howard, Unc!"

Howard began pulling off the disguise, dropping the cane, pushing back the ragged hat from his face, and with a calm and soothing voice asking, "Hey, Unc, remember me? Ha, ha, ha, Unc, remember me now, Unc?"

As Howard drew closer to the addled, totally confused Unc, he shed his remaining costume and smiled nervously. Then, finally, at arm's length and surrounded by all of us, Unc recognized Howard. At once, the old man's eyes grew even larger and angrier. His face swelled, and the huffing growl grew into the sound of a banshee's wail as he turned slowly in a circle, railing out and making little demonic scratching gestures at each of us around him as we tried to calm him, because he knew he had been fooled and he was terribly mad about being duped. He was embarrassed by the scene and felt ridiculous that he hadn't recognized the incorrigible Howard. What had started out as a big surprise for Unc turned out to be a great big surprise for everybody, and we all took our tongue-lashing and dressing-down from the old man as we patted him on his shoulders and tried to massage him with soothing words. Directly Unc responded by ending his frenzy and accepting his role as patsy in the farce Howard had created, and he began hugging Howard and shaking his head in agreement with what anyone was saying, giggling now, and on his way to full recovery. He nestled back down in his snug easy chair, glad to be alive, fully exorcized and happy as a clam. For many years, Dad and Howard revisited the story of Unc, laughing and giggling like pranksters every time the event was retold. When Howard left the ranch that afternoon, he took the wayward pup with him, promising to find him a good home with a wonderful family with a big backyard. And we all were laughing and musing, hoping for a big backyard with a whole lot of trees, and no vegetable garden.

Howard loved his family and relatives, and had a nickname for every one of them: Curly-haired Sally was "Ratsy," Pete was "Cuz," I was "Birdlegs" for obvious reasons, sister Joy was "Topo," a Spanish term meaning "little gopher," and my older sister, Lois, was "Owl," for her big inquisitive eyes. In Howard's own family, his daughter Charlotte was "Seedo," his son Gary was "Butch," his son Rodney was "Rattoon," and his wife, Blanche, respectfully, was "Mama." Even the nickname "Unc" was Howard's creation. These monikers persisted well into later years, and everyone knew precisely who you meant when using them. What was odd is that no one else used any other nicknames in the entire family except those that Howard gave us at a very early age, and they are still used today, hanging on like family relics. This was Howard's innate ability to describe a personality, an entire person, with just a single word, and nail down that impression in everyone's memory forever. This was wrought by his efficiency of thought and incredible power of description.

He loved relaxing with his family, truly setting aside the bustle of business, perhaps cooing and chortling a small baby on his lap, or petting asleep a tiny old Chihuahua coiled up by his side, while he chatted and recalled the day's triumphs and travails with an even, calm manner, unruffled and satisfied, ensconced with loved ones and sharing moments of laughing and family reflection. This was Howard's finest hour. It was a time to acquiesce in a cozy chair, maybe play a game of gin rummy, and get reacquainted with his family after a long day. When on business trips, he always tried to stay with family, where he felt more comfortable and at ease than lodging in a fancy hotel suite, which he could easily afford. But Howard preferred to take the whole adopted family out for a nice steak dinner, then back to the house for a little chatting and off to bed for an early morning rise. Howard was an early riser and most everyone in the family shared his "make hay while the sun shines" mentality; this trait was not genetic but was born out of necessary work. There was never an exact time to arise, but it was always early, and Howard was punctual. Later that day he might show up with twenty-four 16-ounce rib-eye steaks, aged to perfection, delicious beyond description, wrapped up neatly and frozen, enough meat to fill the freezer for a month, compliments of Cuyamaca Meats, Howard's packing house on the outskirts of San Diego. A giving man, no one was more generous than Howard in sharing his prosperity with those he loved, the myriad of people he employed, and their families living on both sides of the border. He hired his best employees with handshakes—no contracts, no promises, just loyalty and honesty, bonds of men that lasted for lifetimes, and everyone was richer. He yearly gave huge parties with many invited, important guests, and right alongside them were Howard's workers, cowboys, and *vaqueros* pitching in as invited guests and cooking, serving, hosting in perfect harmony and unison his famous, fantastic western parties. Everybody was happy then, glad to be invited and working as a team for their beloved *patron,* Howard. He loved and respected these workers and provided for them just like his own family, because they were honest, dedicated, industrious people who believed, like Howard, that caring for others was caring for yourself. I was fortunate to have him as family, and blessed to have known him as a man, with his unselfish example and his hands-on guidance. He was my favorite uncle.

2

Pete

Pete was the nucleus of the three cousins, and he demonstrated his devotion to the extended family throughout his life. His mother died when he was nine years old, and with ten brothers and sisters to tend and nurture, Frank, his father, was hard-pressed to provide all that was necessary for his family. Frank worked at various jobs—hay baling, threshing grain, most of it done manually with mule teams pulling heavy equipment. It was hard, tedious work, with long hours and little money, and now it was necessary for the extended family to help with the children, to feed and send them to school. There was no welfare in those days, just soup kitchens and bread lines, and the kids had to be cared for. Family had to care for family, and the situation loomed even worse with the coming worldwide depression. Pete lived with Amy and Orville, loved them as parents and worked at whatever ranch- or farm-work was necessary. Pete loved his father, but he loved Amy and Orville even more. They gave him a home when he really needed it, and Pete never forgot the love Howard's family showed him. Frank lived into his nineties, preferring solitary living in a trailer under tall Eucalyptus trees in a large grove on Daley property—a toothless, crusty, and twisted old stump of a man tending to his dogs, chewing and spitting Beechnut tobacco out on the ground, at peace, and away from the advancing society surrounding him. It was a perfect hermitage for him. Pete was different. He advanced and prospered with the times. Frank did not, and was not a role model for Pete, who was a modern, efficient thinker and doer who relished new ideas, progress and technology. Pete was an innovative, gifted salesman of what he produced, and a charmer at large with an ability to arrange things, keep workers enthused and accomplish the day's tasks. He loved to work, and for many years it was work with the extended family interests, properties and investments.

The cousins—Pete, Howard, and Lawrence—spent many wonderful years together traversing the treacherous mountain road between San Diego and the Imperial Valley, back and forth, to spend time or work with one another while growing up during a depression that swamped the entire nation in a malaise of desperation and futility. The young men were tough, resourceful, well-known and respected, and when they were not working they could be enjoying themselves at the town hall dances held every Saturday; all three were eligible bachelors who mingled well and were excellent dancers, but Pete fancied himself the best dancer on the floor. He and never failed to amaze the ladies with his quick-step and sharp wit. It was the practice at the dances that at times the ladies would "clap out" their favorite dancer: stand before him and ask, sometimes beg, for a dance by clapping in front of him and then dancing with him. Sally was sixteen when she first clapped for Pete, and of course he responded by dancing with the pretty but too-young-to-court little lady. However, two years later—and having not seen Sally for a while—when she appeared out of nowhere at a dance and clapped him onto the floor, it was a much more mature, improved Sally who enrapt Pete, and instantly they fell in love. But there was a fly in the ointment; Lawrence wanted to court Sally, too, and thought he'd make a better beau than the smaller Pete. But according to Howard, Pete warned him just once.

"Hey, you big, bellowing turd-of-misery, you keep your hands off her!" That ended the discussion about Sally's dating. Lawrence accepted his unacceptability and graciously, wisely bowed out, Sally not having it any other way.

Pete was a compassionate man, rescued from poverty at an early age and given love and sustenance; he felt an urge to help any good, honest person who needed a hand up. When Pete and Sally were first married he was working on the crew digging the All American Canal, earning one dollar a day, and they lived in a tent provided by his employer, suffering the sweltering summer. The work was moving countless tons of dirt and sand with mule teams pulling excavators in the hot valley desert during the middle of the great depression. Their tent was divided in half by a mosquito net, and they were asleep in the back when early in the morning Pete heard a noise at the front of the tent and saw a huge man entering through the flap.

"What do you want?" Pete shouted out, waking Sally.

"My kids are hungry, mister, and I'm hungry," came the grim reply.

"There's a loaf of bread on top of the icebox, take it and leave now!" Pete warned.

"Thank you, mister. God bless you, I'm sorry," he uttered as he snatched the loaf, darted back through the flap and melted into the shadows of the tent city. The times were desperate. Pete later said he would have given him more, but the lone loaf of bread was all the food in the tent. Pete always helped good people at troubled times and this was evident after Orville suffered a stroke and was many years in recovery. Pete tended to him as much as possible, walking him, holding him up, pushing the wheelchair many miles, building him a ramp, driving him, assisting in the bathroom, and doing anything he could do to make Orville's last days more comfortable. Pete was always giving, expecting nothing in return, handing out pure thankfulness and love for all he had received. His gift to everyone was his charitable, hands-on, compassionate spirit.

Lawrence loved Pete and respected him from early childhood onward because Pete was smarter and also would stand toe-to-toe with him physically and not cede an inch to the bigger man. Whether Pete ever whipped Lawrence or simply had a good bluff in, didn't matter. Lawrence never tried to intimidate Pete or ever raised his voice at him, which was certainly not the case with other people. Pete was Lawrence's best friend, but if the big man ever needed to be taken to the woodshed, Pete—out of love for Lawrence—would take him aside and try to straighten him out. In 1962, Pete, Sally, and family were living and working in Vista, with the kids attending school, six miles inland from the coast in Southern California, a snug, tranquil little town in the foothills of the southern Sierra Nevada Mountain Range, population 11,000. It was a wonderful place to grow up. Pete and Sally were successful and prospering in the retail business when Lawrence asked Dad to go to work for him in the Daley Enterprises, a division of the big corporation Lawrence and his brother, Donald, inherited and ran successfully for many years. Pete's first love was his family and second was his work, especially working outside with livestock and farming operations. Lawrence's offer was too enticing—a chance to do work he loved, with greater rewards for his family—and he accepted the job offer.

The next fourteen years were idyllic living on the Bernardo ranch. Pete oversaw the five ranches while Sally earned her real-estate license, and became a broker with a prosperous business and office in the area. The children were educated, lived and sometimes worked on the ranches during school breaks, then eventually married and moved away. Pete was continually busy with projects, and now had a small stable of horses, which he and the family rode often for work and pleasure. There was always work: work on holidays, work on the weekends, and long hours were normal but acceptable if you were doing what you love and enjoy, and Pete relished his duties and responsibilities. But hard work wouldn't stem the increasing onslaught of population and pressure to put the land economically into a higher and better use; it was time to build roads and houses, not to grow barley and graze cattle. Pete's responsibilities for farming and animal husbandry were steadily dwindling as more and more of the ranch acreage was taken for development, and Pete was facing early retirement with the Daley Enterprises, a situation he couldn't abide. Pete doing what at age 62? Sitting idly on the porch in a rocking chair, chewing on a straw and whittling sticks? Retirement was out of the question. There was, however, another option for Pete, and that was moving to southern New Mexico and managing a large ranch that Howard had purchased in the early seventies, in which Lawrence soon bought a half-interest. Although it meant leaving the San Diego area, the land where both he and Sally had grown up and lived for many years, and it would require Sally to relocate her real estate business, they decided to move east and manage the big ranch. It was a prudent but bittersweet decision for them, having to leave a lifetime of friends and family. So eagerly, but somewhat sadly, they packed, loaded trailers with horses and belongings, and in 1975 moved to the Corralitos Ranch, west of Las Cruces, to begin a new ranching assignment. It was one of the wisest decisions Mother and Dad ever made, and it began the happiest, most productive seven years of their lives.

3

The Corralitos

The Corralitos Ranch, during Pete's tenure as ranch manager, was a sprawling, desert highland, 191,000 acres of Federal, State, and private grazing land mixed together and situated at 4,000 feet elevation in southeastern New Mexico in the foothills of the Rocky Mountains. The ranch's southern boundary had, at one time, an international customs station on its border with Mexico before the Gadsden Purchase by the United States in 1853, after which the border was moved 50 miles to the south. The railroad now borders the southern half of the ranch. Heading a line due north from the railroad tracks, with the Aden Hills to the east, the ranch crosses 15,000 acres of scrubby dunes of windblown sand and greasewood brush; then it encompasses fifteen miles of interstate freeway that runs through the ranch east to west; finally it sweeps along broad Mason draw, blanketed with nutritious Grama and tufted Tabosa grasses, crosses the faint remnant of the famed Butterfield Stage route, eventually spanning 25 miles, gaining 2,400 feet in elevation, and ending at the base of craggy, cracking Magdalena Peak, a stark, giant extrusion of shattered shale, huge red chunks of jagged volcanic boulders, and metamorphic rock soaring to 6,600 feet on the northern border. To the west along that line lies a third of the ranch, rolling pastureland dotted with mesquite, chemise brush, and greasewood, the land carved by occasional torrential summer monsoon flash floods, cutting deep arroyos gouged out from the base of the Sierra de Las Uvas Mountains surrounding Magdelena Peak, and forming the northwestern ranch boundary.

Further southwest, the Uvas blend into a rolling, rugged high mesa, rich in loamy, sandy soil, an excellent pasture extending to the southwestern ranch boundary, six miles south of Interstate 10. The eastern two-thirds of the Corralitos is split in half by north-south hills spanning from Magdalena Peak to the interstate freeway. The sweeping vista from the Rough and Ready highest mesa on the north east slopes is stunning, spectacular, looking east over four miles of fertile Hawkins pasture. In the distance rises Robledo Mountain and its foothills, dotted with natural caverns and 1800s silver mines, forming the northeast ranch boundary; the hills trail back into the low, fertile valley four miles wide and run six miles to the south, dropping in elevation and forming its basin at the Ranch headquarters, which was built higher up on the slopes of the Sleeping Lady Hills to avoid flooding. This valley forms a large playa lake two miles wide and seven miles long when inundated by a heavy summer downpour of monsoon rain, which can fill the basin in less than an hour, and producing a fertile high yielding pasture when dry. From the same high mesa in the Rough and Ready, to the east 2,000 feet below, spreads out the Mesilla Valley, carved by the Rio Grande River eons past. The valley encompasses the city of Las Cruces, which is surrounded by the Dona Ana Mountains to the north and bound on the east by the erupting, towering granite spires of the Organ Mountains punching through the bedrock and rising to 9,000 feet. The view fades away following the course of the river into the distant haze of El Paso and Juarez, sixty miles to the southeast in this fertile, robust valley. It is picture-postcard scenery from this high vantage on the Rough and Ready, and few but seasoned hikers or cowboys chasing strays have ever seen it because of its isolation. From the headquarters, sweeping to the southeast are hummocks of sand and mesquite stuck and mired together, stuffed with chemise brush and cholla cactus, and forming prickly, brushy, organic dunes ten feet high, huge humps of vegetative sand immovable except by bulldozer. The growth provides edible beans and flowers, and the sandy soil germinates hundreds of species of weeds that cattle will readily graze and thrive on after a half inch of rain blankets the area during the warmer seasons in a high desert, grateful for any moisture. The sandy hummocks surround the Las Cruces Airport and gradually blend into the southeastern ranch boundary, an escarpment carved out by the Rio Grande and dropping 800 feet into the valley. To the south of the headquarters, the ranch crosses four miles of sandy washes slicing in from the Sleeping Lady Hills, traverses the East Gap pasture covered with edible, brushy forage and native grasses, then passes Reichey Butte, a huge, shattered plug of purple granite rock bursting through the sand, and breaking up into chunks and fragments as it rises 350 feet above the desert floor to the summit. Angular and jagged, impossible to graze, the pinnacle is accessible only by experienced rock climbers, and with crumbling sharp shards of rock, is a dangerous ascent even for them. Heading south the ranch passes again over the freeway and sweeps into the volcanic fields, loamy sand, and cinder cones of the southeast pasture, butting up against the West Potrillo Mountains and Aden Hills, comprising 27,000 acres, which adjoins neighboring ranches and forms the southern boundary of the Corralitos.

This was the Corralitos Ranch, raw and—except for fencing—virtually untouched land that Pete would improve and make more productive. In the late 1800s it was a large, rocky, verdant patch of land in a disputed territory in the northern Chihuahua Desert, bordering a big turbulent river of life-giving water. It was a land filled with war, hardship, and bloody drama. The territory fought over by Mexico and the United States was infested with gringo rustlers and Mexican banditos, frequented by back-shooting, punk gunslingers. It was also plagued by a marauding, slaughtering band of Chiracahua Apaches, led by war chief Victorio, who rebelled against their resettlement, fled the reservation and created havoc for emigrants and families crossing the land on horses, wagons, and stagecoaches. Ownership of land was ultimately determined by who could defend it with weapons. It was a haven for a caboodle of dangerous social misfits who created rampant lawlessness in the wild, untamed region bordering two countries that was patrolled only by a handful of lawmen and a small cavalry of soldiers: valiant but overwhelmed men. In the ensuing decades, with the coming of the railroads in the 1870s and wave after wave of westward emigration, the lawlessness subsided. So when New Mexico achieved statehood in 1912, and after its land survey in the 1940s, the land ultimately was parceled out into private, state, and federal ownership; the private land was then tied together with state leases and federal grazing permits to form numerous ranches, the Corralitos being one of the largest. This was the land that Pete was to subdue and perfect, not with guns and treaties but with seasoned cowboys, loyal Mexican ranch hands, a gifted insight, and a large bulldozer. This was Pete's finest hour.

Pete and Sally's first task arriving at the ranch, after temporarily storing their possessions and stabling their horses, was to rehabilitate the headquarters and the old ranch house, a rambling one-story adobe structure. They rented an apartment in Las Cruces for two months during the headquarters fix-up, and commuted forty miles back and forth every day during the renovation. The old house had been built and rebuilt over a seventy-five year period with former owners and caretakers adding a flourish here and there. The basic structure and foundation was still sound, just in need of a new roof, some carpentry repair work, new paint, a face-lift for the swimming pool, and a general clean-up of the house and the grounds inside the thick adobe perimeter fence. Intruding, thorny mesquite trees were cut down; tumbleweeds, which in numbers can be tinderboxes for fires, had blown in and piled up against fence lines surrounding the headquarters, barns, and corrals. They were heaped up with pitchforks in open areas and burned quickly under a watchful eye on a windless day. The living compound was one of four structures: the main house, a cook house, a guest quarters, and a bar and billiards room that was built in the late fifties by Dorrance Roderick, former owner of the ranch and of the *El Paso Times*. The big room housed the Luke Short Back Bar, a historic old bar built in the 1880s, a silent witness of countless shadowy characters, high-stakes card games, whisky shots, brawls, and gunfights. The adobe barroom was built with a high ceiling especially to house the legendary bar with its ornate mirror, hand-carved frame, and marble pillar posts chipped by stray bullets. The bar filled half a wall and stood nine feet high. Pete connected the main house, the bar, and guesthouse with a large living area and atrium that held out the weather, then installed a big wood-burning fireplace that made the new enclosure warm and comfortable. Only the cookhouse stood alone, with its meat-hanging cooler, band saws, ovens, stoves, and a fifteen-foot-long dining table that, when in use, fed hungry crews of ranch hands three hearty meals daily.

The horse barn, the equipment barn and the shop were reroofed, and a bunkhouse that could sleep ten men was restored to a habitable condition. Three small houses for the foreman and cowboys were improved and made more livable. A ten-acre permanent pasture and sprinkling system was put in around the headquarters, and all of the fence lines, posts, and gates were straightened, tightened, and repaired. Pete's work was a marvel of rejuvenation with his small crew of half a dozen workers, and for two months Sally drove tirelessly hauling in supplies for the project by pickup from Las Cruces and El Paso, fully as dedicated as Pete. Lawrence and Howard were happy, very pleased with the results and generous in their support of the updates, and Pete was thrilled to do the work. Within six weeks he and Sally moved into the renovated, rambling, 7,200-square-foot main house, and with a spruced-up headquarters, together, dauntless, they began another exciting ranching project.

Water is the ultimate resource, the universal solvent, a necessity. Without it nothing gets done. It is more vital than sunshine and more valuable than all the world's wealth, so precious we have drilled thousands of feet into the earth in search of it, and explored the surface of the moon looking for it. Likewise, everything productive on the Corralitos was ultimately tied to water. All the people, cattle, crops, and livelihoods depended on available, potable water coming from the rain, snow, or underground wells. A sustainable source of water was the primary concern of the rancher in the high, semi-arid desert, and was sought after and protected even when plentiful, fought over and coveted when scarce. Early settlers on the high mesa of the Corralitos hauled water from the Rio Grande in barrels with mule teams, 1,000 feet up the treacherous switch-back wagon track carved from the escarpment up from the valley below—hard, grueling, never-ending water hauling that made homesteading possible. Water windmills were developed in the late 1800s to supply water for the railroad's insatiable steam engines that needed dependable water refill stations at points along the route west. But the savage desert wind gusts at 90 miles per hour would destroy the inner pumping parts of the windmills; breakdowns were frequent and they needed constant attention. In 1888, Aeromotor Company, to satisfy the water need of the railroads, built and patented a windmill with a centrifugal clutch that would shut off in high winds and protect the pumping mechanism 200 feet deep underground. This phenomenal, beneficial invention greatly aided the railroads' push westward. It provided life-giving water and was the beginning of improvement of the vast, arid Mojave, a dry wind-blown desert between the Rocky Mountains and the Pacific Ocean. Ranchers soon began using the dependable pumps to provide livestock water in otherwise inaccessible areas, spreading out their pasturage, allowing more animals to graze. For many years windmills were the only dependable source of water for the outer pastures of the Corralitos, and were a blessing for ranching and wildlife alike.

Pete's ongoing task at the Corralitos was to improve the water resources: the windmills, cattle drinkers, earthen tanks, and farm irrigation. He loved working with water and was fit for the task, having engineered and worked with wells, dams, pipelines and sprinkling systems in all sorts of applications for the

Daley Enterprises in California. On the Corralitos, one of his first jobs was to repair old cattle-water pipelines and lay new lines where necessary, connecting the new lines with the windmills and drinkers, installing new drinkers where none had existed before, then interconnecting the water lines with valves to divert and share water when necessary. This was a large, expansive undertaking, and of over 80 miles of existing pipeline, 50 miles had to be repaired or replaced by new, strong PVC pipelines. They were laid in two-foot-deep furrows bladed out by a 1940s-vintage road grader, an old, serviceable, useful piece of equipment that Howard provided. Wherever an old section of line had a continual problem with leaks, it was replaced. In the rocky spots where the grader couldn't blade, the furrows were picked and shoveled out by hand by Pete's crew, normally just a few vigorous, hard-working ranch hands. Windmill wells were cleaned out and some deepened to increase water supply; electric submersible pumps were installed in the ground wells and in the windmills' above-ground storage tanks, wherever electricity was available. Storage tanks were grouted and sealed inside to prevent leaking. Bullet holes on the sides of the tanks, shot by thoughtless vandals, were plugged. Leaks in water lines throughout the ranch were sought out and fixed, for even small leaks were capable of draining out hundreds of gallons of precious water onto the ground in a single day. There were thirteen windmills and fifteen storage tanks, most holding 5-10,000 gallons apiece, sometimes using old railroad tank cars for storage, and many drinkers were spread throughout eleven pastures to supply water for almost 300 square miles of grazing land. Some of these drinkers were base drinkers, a name assigned by the Bureau of Land Management; these watering locations established the grandfathered legal right enacted under the Taylor Grazing Act of 1934, to provide water, pay a fee, and graze cattle on public land. The base drinkers had to be supplied with potable water at all times or the permit to graze could be revoked, again stressing the importance of water ownership and stewardship. In one craggy canyon at the bottom of Magdelena Peak was a base drinker that had to be supplied with water from a lower well across a huge 21,000-acre, rocky pasture stretching five miles to the south, the well sunk in a large arroyo at the Adobe corrals. A combination of pumps, using both butane and diesel, were rigged together to suck the water from the ground and pump it uphill for five miles to the base holding tank. It was a cantankerous set-up of piston-pumps, tanks, valves, and piping, all subject to freezing, situated in a sharp, rocky soil creating many leaks, and constantly needing repair. A submersible pump could have been put in the well and would have solved many problems, but, unfortunately, the nearest source of electricity was six miles to the south, so the antiquated pumping system had to be maintained to supply the base drinker even though it was very costly and labor intensive. But the requirements of the grazing permit were fulfilled, and the base drinker always had water or was under repair to provide water. Water was always the coveted possession on the ranch, and Pete employed one full-time worker with a four-wheel-drive truck to find leaks, dig them out, fix them, and regulate the cattle water system throughout the vast pastures. It was never-ending work, and just the beginning of Pete's conquest of water on the Corralitos.

I moved to the ranch in the spring of 1976 from California at age 31, after attending college and spending seven years doing sales and nutritional work with feed yards in the southwest. I worked for a fine company with wonderful people, but the job required constant traveling, something I disliked and never got used to. After a recent divorce, I needed a change in thinking, attitude, and geography, and I decided I would move to the Corralitos and work for the family on the large ranch. My two children, Pete and Gretchen, whom I loved and supported, stayed in the capable hands of their mother in California. It was the smartest move in my life, for I not only received work, love, and the acceptance of family, but I found what I really needed: sobriety, and that made all the difference. I loved returning to the ranching life. I had lived it growing up, and it was always calling me to return, beckoning me back. Now I was living it again, helping Pete, Howard, and Lawrence with their projects and cattle. It was the greatest growing and learning experience in my life.

There was constant activity at the headquarters. Work began at seven, and if there were no emergencies, ended around five. But necessary work took priority and no one rested until the horses were fed and the compound was cleaned up and orderly, weekends no exception. Four to five families, as many as fifteen adults and children, worked on the ranch, living at the headquarters in three separate houses, two mobile homes, and a large bunkhouse for the single men. Everyone grew gardens. Some meat was supplied; there was always an old cow or steer fattening in the corrals to slaughter to help feed the crew, and the freezers were stocked with deer meat during the hunting season. We pumped our own water and stored our own gas, diesel, and propane delivered from town for the trucks, equipment, and dwellings. Along with propane stoves, there were cords of mesquite firewood to warm the houses. A school bus picked up the children; it maneuvered the hazardous nine-mile trip back and forth from the freeway on a narrow, high-banked county road spanning the headquarters and the freeway. But there was no newspaper delivery or mail box, so all correspondence had to be picked up at the post office fifteen miles away down the same perilous road, the lifeline of the ranch. At the headquarters there were always things to fix and look after. Most of the electrical, mechanical repair, and upkeep was done by Pete's crew, including overseeing the domestic water supply that was stored in a large tank at the main house. Outside contractors were hired occasionally, but normally they were too expensive, too far away, and too slow to respond. Every family sustained itself, but we looked after each other because of common interests and safety, and Pete was the final arbitrator in any dispute.

Industrious Sally, in addition to her responsibilities at the ranch, bought and renovated an old home in an uptown section of Las Cruces, population 65,000 and growing. She turned it into a real estate office, obtained her broker's license, hired two full-time sales people, and began dealing houses and properties in the robust, expanding real estate market in the Mesilla Valley. As she commuted to town daily for her business, she would haul supplies back to the ranch in her favorite vehicle, a pickup; she was always ready to assist in any of Pete's projects, buying groceries for the bunkhouse crew, or doing emergency runs to El Paso for hard-to-find parts. Mother was a constant blur of energy, never wavering, never tiring, constantly improving everyone's circumstance, and making a perfect pack mule, mail carrier, and liaison between the ranch and the city. She loved her duties and was so accomplished at getting things done; work to Mother resulted in a purposeful, rewarding life, and she and Dad working together were very happy in their new surroundings, anticipating new projects together, and still very much alive and very much in love.

Pete's other love, water, was still beckoning him—if not water from underground wells, then water spread out behind a wide earthen dam like the one he was heaping up in an arroyo to catch and tame run-off rain deluges. Pete's ally in his capturing of Corralitos ground water was Howard's bulldozer, a construction-sized tracklayer that weighed 35 tons with dozer attached. In the hands of an experienced operator it was an effective and efficient earth-mover. With each pass, the powerful tractor would inch up the inside of the dam and push nine cubic yards of fresh earth to add to the top of the structure. He watched the big bulldozer excavating tons of dirt in a single bite of the blade, pushing it from the bottom of the arroyo basin to the top of the dam and dropping the load there. He carefully checked his transit for proper height and leveling of the growing structure, which could be 100 yards long, 25 feet wide at the top, 75 feet wide at the base, and 30 feet deep at the basin bottom when finished. But the most important step in building the dam Pete had already taken, deciding where along the arroyo channel to erect the dam and build the spillway. The dam had to capture as much water as possible and not back up onto county roads or encroach upon historic sites. It would need an area where a durable spillway could be built, preferably in the narrow of an arroyo sided by rocky structure to blend in, raise and attach the dam, then build the spillway over a hard rocky spot to prevent washouts, because without a proper spillway the dam could be washed over and swept away with the first monsoon torrent of rain. As Pete watched the tractor and perused the project, he was very happy with the construction progress and completing work on time.

When first building the dam, the initial job for the bulldozer was to remove all the vegetation from the area surrounding the dam site. The useless brush was dozed aside. Then the mesquite was knocked down and pushed into a separate pile for a few days of drying. Later it was run over and crushed by the heavy tractor, breaking the tall, hardy mesquite into smaller burnable chunks of firewood, no chain saw needed. The wood was then loaded on a flat rack truck, hauled to the compound, and used to heat the houses. The earthen dam needed to be free of most of the decomposing organic matter or the dam would not pack down properly; it would be compromised by providing an easy, safe harborage for rodents, badgers and other critters digging dens and burrows, which would damage the dam. It had to be air-tight with no leaks, especially along the bottom of the structure, which was subject to greater water pressure due to depth. After clearing away the brush, the tractor would begin to hollow out a depression in the arroyo bed, forming the water basin, the tank of the dam. All the excavated earth was pushed up to the inside face of the growing dam site and spread out on top, adding to the height of the dam. The heavy, rumbling dozer packed down the earth, adding fresh earth with each pass, running over the back and front of the dam, tamping, forming, packing and daubing the growing structure like a giant, industrious mud-wasp building its nest from the materials at hand. The perfect combination of dam material was sand, small rocks, adobe clay, and fragmented shale all blended and molded while shaping the dam, then relentlessly packed down by the big dozer. Pete surveyed the progress inch by inch, examining the consistency, height, and width of the structure daily. When completed with a proper spillway, and full, the dam could back up water for a half-mile and capture 25 million gallons of the precious liquid, enough to hold water in the tank for a year or more. While sprouting numerous edible plants and mossy ecosystems along its banks, it provided livestock and wildlife with water year round. It would contain 6,000 tons of earth and capture a large lake full of water, a bountiful resource in a hot, dry desert, a man-made oasis, and Pete's gift to fauna and flora alike.

The big dozer needed a small back-up crew to maintain it while on site or moving to another of the numerous remote dam projects. Fuel for the tractor was hand-pumped daily from a mobile refueling tank towed to the site by a pickup loaded with grease, oil, water, and an assortment of wrenches, bars and heavy-duty jacks to service the tractor. Gordo, the Mexican operator and caretaker of the tractor, serviced it daily and maintained it in top condition. He was Pete's counterpart in tractor work, much like Howard's loyal mechanic, Frank, at the feed yard, who built Howard's chutes. Gordo was an ace at dirt work with a bulldozer in treacherous terrain, a keen-eyed master at the controls, and Pete's right-hand man in his construction and farming projects. Howard would also run parts from California in his own pickup, more than 1,100 miles round trip, to repair the tractor, and when necessary send a factory mechanic to the ranch to keep the tracklayer in excellent shape. Howard loved things working properly and was an immense help to Pete keeping the bulldozer and other equipment serviced and productive in such a remote location. With a top-notch dozer, Pete would continually build and repair 52 dam sites on the Corralitos, some of them twenty miles apart, scattered throughout the eleven large pastures on the ranch. This work established a precedent for eventual ownership of the ground water captured when later the water-rights issue would be addressed in the New Mexico legislature and public forums.

The bulldozer dirt work was always a focal point and gathering spot when

Lawrence and Howard came to the ranch on their frequent visits. On one occasion, all four of us squashed together on the bench seat of my pickup and drove out to inspect a new dam site. When we arrived, the men got out and slowly climbed the packed dirt to the top of the growing dam, scuffing the fresh, aromatic earth with their boots, absorbing the sounds, smells, and ground-rumbling growl of the powerful tractor. It grunted, clacked, pushing and sighing, then belched black smoke that thickened the air as the tractor gathered tons of freshly turned soil to add to the top of the dam. They were relishing the experience as they watched the dozer slice off thick ribbons of red earth to push up the incline, chatting back and forth, poking fun and chiding each other, chortling, giggling, bellowing, echoing laughter so loud that it momentarily silenced the roar of the tractor.

Then, enrapt in the merriment, the happy, reveling inspectors turned and ambled across the spine of the dam like three kids adventuring along a train track. Howard halted mid-way to point out two black bulls fighting down below the dam, 50 yards away, butting heads, spinning in circles like a rotary mower, cracking down brush, scattering cows and calves and kicking up rocks and dust into a cloud. The cousins watched the bullfight from above, laughing, ribbing each other, picking their favorite bull, while hoping that neither animal broke a leg or ribs in the fracas. Then from the side, in a flash, a huge, horned Brahman bull, which was watching the fight close by, entered the scuffle by attacking and viciously butting the smaller black bull in the shoulders, knocking it down, then butting it as it got up, sending both black bulls fleeing, pawing and scuffling, scattering the dirt to get out of harm's way, and stopping the brutal conflict. The fight ended exactly as it should have: the winner took all, and size did matter. Hitting from behind was okay, and two against one was better. Those are the rules for a bullfight, and the men thoroughly enjoyed it. It was gratifying to see the three men I loved and admired finding so much pleasure out in the open air on their own range land, engrossed in a mutual project, and after so many years, feeling the same loving companionship, closeness, and family unity. I was happy and proud to be a working part and share in this feeling of belonging and importance.

The saga of these three men and their successes would not have happened without the wives who shared their lives. Their spouses were responsible for the direction and stability of these resourceful men, and these women enriched their husbands' productivity. They were the rudders of the big boats, the yeast in the dough, the homemakers and the peacemakers. There was Sally, my mother, ever ready and up to any task, single-minded in her devotion to Pete, dynamic in action, and dogged with determination. She would tackle any work asked of her for unity of the ranching family. She was shrewd in business, could not be fooled, and was just as capable of riding horseback alongside veteran cowboys gathering cattle as she was writing a real-estate contract at her desk in the headquarters. She was a magnificent, loving mother and a doer of all things.

And there was Lawrence's wife Bertha, of Scandinavian descent, beautifully proportioned, sculpted and hardened by physical activity, strong—a skilled horsewoman with thousands of hours of experience in the saddle gathering livestock. She often tended to me in my childhood and was loving, attentive, and protective like my mother—a marvelous second mom. She and Sally in most things were as close as sisters. They kept secrets and looked after each other for many years. A generous, happy woman, saddened at times only by the emotional turmoil of living with a belittling, bellicose husband. She had to be dedicated, resilient, and in love to live with this obstinate man.

Then there was my aunt Blanche, strikingly beautiful, a knockout, adorned with shining jet-black hair. She was petite, but diminutive in size only. Early on she was my confidant, my friend, a warm shoulder to cry on. She was a great, experienced listener who would listen and then advise me on all my complaints and rumblings about working for the family, the long hours of harvesting barley, dusty, itching work, with little time off, while the other kids enjoyed the beach. And she coached me with skills to cope with Lawrence, my constant nemesis, boss and overseer. A mighty-might, a feisty little woman, Aunt Blanche told you what she thought and felt, then stood her ground, eye to eye. Having two boys herself, she understood young men and also the entire extended family situation I was caught up and entangled in. She was, often in my late teens and beyond, my wise advisor and my port in the storm. She was as good, as trustworthy, and as loving as an aunt could be, and I was fortunate to be included in her clutch of kids.

This, then, was the triad of women—Sally, Bertha, and Blanche, the epitome of femininity and toughness, the trinity of direction and unity on the Corralitos. Remarkable women, they were devoted to their husbands, being drawn together into a family of men, raising children, running businesses, settling disputes, adapting to whatever, taking charge, getting things done and solving problems. I never heard them fight or squabble among themselves, although in private away from the men they no doubt had a spat or two, but they were much too wise to air their differences any further than their circle of three. When they organized any ranch activity together it worked like clockwork, and their leadership, many times behind the scenes, was essential to the operation of the Corralitos.

Another leader was to join the women soon and then the triad would become a fierce foursome and be complete, and the new attractive addition to the ranching family was my wife, Barbara.

It was December 30, 1978, when I unexpectedly met Barbara in the hacienda patio at the Holiday Inn in Las Cruces. It was a delightful, star-strewn evening in the high desert. The Inn was packed with early revelers anticipating the holiday eve, and as I entered the patio and turned the corner towards the cantina, I recognized Preach, a jovial old man and family friend, sitting with a huge smile smeared on his ruddy, happy face as I approached. And then I saw Barbara, and I knew exactly why Preach had been trying to get us together, and why the old man was now beaming, for beside him sat the most beautiful woman I had ever seen. Preach presented her to me as promised. In the next instant our eyes connected and then there was nothing else in the world but she and me. Those captivating, sparkling green eyes, and that summoning, perfect smile, were enhanced by a flawless olive complexion, and dramatic, well proportioned features. She was outfitted in boots, a snazzy western blouse, a winter pants suit, and her glowing, thick, sable hair outlined her radiant countenance. Her outfit was complemented with rare pieces of native turquoise. A squash-blossom necklace of exceptional quality and beauty adorned her neck, and a glint of diamonds flashed here and there from rings on her shapely, strong fingers. She was dressed to stand out, and she did. As I drew nearer she became even more beautiful, and, oh, those beguiling, beckoning green eyes. She was impossible for me to resist, a temptress of the best sort, and I eagerly spoke, "You must be Barbara."

"And you must be Larry," she nodded back, pointing a beautifully manicured finger at my nose.

I felt at that instant to be the luckiest man alive, ensconced with friends in this warm, inviting atmosphere, and face to face with this shapely, gorgeous lady, being drawn in by her captivating eyes and the waft of her lightly scented body, so enticing, so desirable, everything about her attracting my senses. And at that second I fell inescapably in love and I knew I must have her, that I never wanted this glorious feeling to end, and that Barbara and I should never again be apart.

Barbara sold her home in Dallas in the spring of 1979 and moved 700 miles west from the big city to the Corralitos ranch to live with me. She had lived in Dallas most of her life, and with two busy teenage children living with her ex-husband, and a myriad of friends and treasured memories, it was not an easy decision for her to make. She had to transplant herself from cozy, close-in city living to the rugged, expansive, sometimes hostile and austere conditions of living and working on a high desert cattle ranch. She loved her kids, but she would see them often, never missing special events and holidays; the kids would likewise visit the ranch whenever they could, with direct flights from El Paso to Dallas several times a day facilitating the fun visits. I knew Barbara was making a sea-change in life direction, and I wanted her to be happy, like me. I was humbled and thankful for her positive, loving attitude and the unselfish sacrifice she made in leaving Dallas. Four of us—Mom, Dad, Barbara, and I—packed, boxed, lugged and finally loaded her house full of belongings and furniture into three pickups and a pair of twenty-foot gooseneck stock trailers and left town that afternoon, following the setting sun west. It was a wonderful time and place to be alive, and especially to share it with my wife, my life mate, Barbara.

Barbara was not only beautiful. She was smart and tough, could be sly as a coyote if necessary, and was not an easy mark. Even Lawrence respected her for her ability to hold her own against his bellowing shenanigans that were purposely insulting to me. She was refined, but no prissy lady. Her voice could be as loud and raucous as Lawrence's, and she loved pitching his humiliations back at him, daring him to prove his braggadocio and exposing his vacuous threats, leaving him muttering and stammering. Then, like a perfect lady, she excused herself and sat down happily to play the piano. She knew well the wiles of men; she could tell bawdy tales with the best of them and had called Lawrence's bluff. I was happy, relieved, and very proud of her.

Throughout my earlier years, Lawrence had singled out my teenage girl-friends for his personal welcoming of shock and intimidation, trying to embarrass my young friends for his own enjoyment. This harassment usually happened during branding operations. He belittled with blood and guts: once it was blood and hair he smeared with his finger on the cuff of the designer jeans worn by a cute little friend. Once it was cow crap wiped off his finger onto the shiny, clean, boots of a pretty acquaintance sitting alone on a fence rail. On one occasion at roundup, during a castration operation at the chute, my girlfriend was holding the catch pan for the testicles, so after Lawrence emasculated the calf he could drop the testicles in the pan as quickly and sanitarily as possible. During the operation, which normally goes smoothly and without pause, he momentarily stopped his hand short of the pan, and held the severed testicles aloft, dripping blood and serum onto the forearm and wrist of his pretty helper; Lawrence stood there grinning, proud of himself, hoping for her to wince and cry out in revulsion. But no, with blood running down to her elbow and dripping to the ground, she looked him in the eye and quipped back, "Nice going, Uncle Lawrence, now drop the balls in the bucket and get back to work!" That stunned Lawrence, ridiculed him in front of his friends who were watching the whole scene and laughed heartily. That small retort shut him up, and he never bothered her again.

Likewise, Barbara was too smart, too savvy, and too mature to be intimidated by Lawrence. In one incident inside the headquarters, she was hollering from the washroom that there was a big snake under the clothes dryer. Lawrence rushed in and ordered everyone out of the way, got down on his knees, reached back behind the dryer and pulled out a four-and-a-half-foot bull snake, grabbing it with one hand behind the neck. Then he held it up in front of Barbara, teasing her, shaking the writhing snake in front of her eyes, and bellowing about everyone else being a bunch of sissies. Barbara just stared at him, trying to anticipate his next asinine move, and then Lawrence turned and marched triumphantly out of the house, throwing the snake into the pasture. Barbara wasn't impressed with Lawrence's scare tactics, just happy to get the critter out of the house and to get back to doing the laundry. She certainly could defend herself against the unpredictable Lawrence. As far as keeping him in line, she had the tacit support of all the ranch matriarchs, and for that I was thankful.

Barbara joined a small, but powerful triad of accomplished, resourceful women, and she fit in perfectly and contributed immensely to the Corralitos Ranch. After my mother's maternal acceptance of her new on-site daughter-in-law, Mom grew to love Barbara. Bertha respected and loved her for her handling of Lawrence and her ability to get things done. Barbara and Blanche hit it off immediately, shared the same preferences, pleasures, and mannerisms. They were like closely bonded sisters, separated by age only, and were a matched pair. Together these four dynamic women worked in unison on the essential ranch duties, tending to the family responsibilities, and undertaking yearly the ranch's most important task to which they all would contribute, the roundup: the gathering of the cattle.

4

Roundup

The roundup was the harvest of the calf crop off the ranch. It was a gathering not only of cattle, but of selected friends, families, working cowboys, dudes, groupies, and lovers of horses. It was a time of western camaraderie and delicious, authentic food, a time for work and a time for fun. People traveled from as far as California to attend, a marvelous assortment of guests. The roundup on a working cattle ranch was a huge attraction to the city dwellers, who loved the sights, sounds, and earthy smells of gathering and processing cattle. The folks fortunate enough to be invited were thrilled and awed with the raw intensity and action of roundup, and always begged to come back. We had as many as 25 guests and cowboys, with many horses. Most beds on the ranch were full, and the driveway was lined with motor-homes. City ladies wore flowered hats, sipped a morning mimosa, or wished they had one.

Pete and his crew were busy readying the equipment, barns, horse stables, and the headquarters corrals, prepping the area for an onslaught of cattle and cowboys. Our veterinarian gave nine of the ranch horses a thorough examination, and a farrier was called out to reshoe the horses. Nutritious, freshly cured alfalfa hay was pulled from the lofts and stacked near the mangers in the horse barn, and supplemental sacks of rolled oats were stored in the tack room. The horse stalls were shoveled out and raked down. Wind-blown sand and muck were scraped out of the corral alleys with a tractor, and the gates were cleaned under with shovels, so they swung easily. Vaccines and antibiotics for the livestock were purchased and stored in the headquarters cold room. New tires were mounted on the pickups and trailers, and all the equipment was washed and cleaned. In the holding areas surrounding the compound, posts were straightened and reset, the barbed wire fence lines tightened, and wire gates were straightened out and reworked so they, too, would open easily. Pete's work at the headquarters was progressing well, and even before the roundup began, he started gathering cattle together in the outer pastures, much of the time without any help from the cowboys.

About a month before roundup—and depending on the forage conditions in the pastures—Pete's crew would open and close chosen gates and shut off water sources in certain areas to entice the cattle to move closer to the corrals where they would be processed. It was less stressful on the animals, especially cows with small calves, for them to move on their own instead of being pushed and driven for miles by cowboys during roundup. Bales of fresh alfalfa hay were carried out daily, broken into large flakes, and placed strategically near corrals, gates, and pastures, to lure the cattle to the processing corrals. With the smell of fresh hay in the air wafting many miles, it wouldn't be long before the cows and calves followed their noses, meandered through the gates to different pastures, ate a flake of hay, and headed in the right direction, looking for available water and for more to eat. Eleven large pastures and four sets of corrals were used to process and transport cattle, and Pete would try to relocate the cattle in five or six pastures surrounding these working corrals; he hoped there would be enough forage in these holding pastures to sustain the cattle a few weeks before roundup. Roundup was costly, as it meant weight loss and stress on the herd, so gathering was tailored to strategies that were best for the cattle. About eighty percent of the herd in the outer pastures could be gathered without using the cowboys, but later Pete would have to sweep these pastures with the ranch cowboys on horses to clean up the straggling cattle and push them closer to the pastures around the working corrals. When Pete was done with this pre-roundup work, he would have only six pastures to gather rather than eleven, and he had reduced the time, work and cost of the greater roundup.

The first day of the roundup finally arrived. House cars and motor homes lumbered into the headquarters in the afternoon, where they parked along the driveway and were leveled off with blocks. Pickups pulling horse trailers came rattling and clacking the cattle guards as they passed into the compound, and people began unloading horses and mules into the stalls and storing tack in the saddle room. Guests staying in the headquarters unloaded luggage and stowed it in their appointed bedrooms. There was an aura of excitement at headquarters. The back bar was lit up, and happy hour began, with cocktails, friendly exchanges and hugs, and meetings of old and new friends. Shared stories and recollections of past roundups buzzed in the air. The fireplace warmed the back bar, where cowboys and guests were aglow, anxiously anticipating the next few days on horseback on the Corralitos, and the excitement of the revelers and the sounds of a great party coming from the bar escalated to a low roar. Men told horse stories, each with his own tall tale of roundup lore to add to the conversation. Small groups of women stood in the corners and sat on the sofas sipping their hi-balls, chatting incessantly, and exchanging treasured bits of information. Mixed pairs were vying at the shuffleboard and racking up eight-ball games on the pool table. Music filled the room. A daring couple was two-stepping, scooting around in scuffed-up boots on the hardwood floor, dancing to a western jig and trying to dodge both the animated bar crowd and the crouching, cue-stroking pool players. With loud laughter, the entire crew carried on, having their most fun ever. A sense of homecoming and belonging filled the bar, and the atmosphere was exhilarating, totally western, totally cowboy.

Then the aroma of wonderful food wafted in from the cookhouse and through the festive bar—luring, beckoning, and enticing with irresistible scent, and the unquestionable clanging from the cookhouse bell heralded supper being served. Guests began exiting the bar, drinks in hand, ambling toward the cook-house. Trays, bowls, and platters of hot food and fixings filled the smorgasbord: Bertha's succulent roast beef with potatoes, and her savory green salad; Blanche's delicious hominy grits and fresh zucchini squash casseroles; Sally's huge platters of spicy chile rellenos stuffed with creamy Mexican cheese, and a large pot of her trademark ranch-style beans; boatloads of Barbara's zesty gravy and a sweet assortment of her freshly baked cakes and pies. The authenticity, freshness and quantity of food were overwhelming, and the cowboys and guests sat at the long cookhouse table and ate and talked until sated. Some headed back to the bar for a nightcap, while others, travel-weary, went directly to bed. Tomorrow's long, hard day would start early with breakfast before daybreak. The work would begin before sunrise and hopefully end before sunset, but it would be hectic, fast-paced, and dangerous. So for now it was early to bed, preparing to be early to rise after a good night's rest for everyone.

Pete's ranch crew and the hired cowboys finished breakfast and were at the barn before dawn, readying for the roundup. Half the riders were professional cowboys, men who made their living working with horses and cattle. These men would do most of the hard, dirty, necessary roundup work. The other half were the guests, people of varied professions: doctors, lawyers, businessmen, horse enthusiasts, trail riders, and would-be wranglers. But all were friends, and all loved the roundup experience but were greenhorns who lacked the skills of the true cowboy. The cowboys groomed and saddled their own horses so they could assist the guests when they arrived at the barn; they would help saddle the guests' horses, make last-minute fixes to their gear, secure tie-downs, give riding sugges-tions, assist the novice riders in any way, and outfit them to gather cattle. Some of the cowboys were brought in from different areas; some had their own ranches or worked on ranches. Some worked in the California feedlots full time and earned extra money working roundups on different ranches. Lawrence and Howard had skilled Mexican cowboys traveling with them, assisting wherever they worked cattle. These Mexican cowboys were raised on ranches from childhood and lived with their horses in the barns, sometimes inside the stalls caring for their animals. These healthy, happy, robust young men were the animals' midwives, nursemaids, trainers, and constant companions. This was a Mexican tradition and a family business, a livelihood handed down through generations, and their early boyhood training produced some of the finest cowboys and hands-on stockmen in the world, so these cowboys were coveted and employed by both Mexican and American ranch owners for their expertise wrangling livestock. The other cowboys were just as capable, for most of them had spent most of their working lives on horseback, tending, gathering and processing livestock. All of them had many years of experience.

Before sunrise, the ten cowboys and eleven greenhorn guests loaded their horses and two mules in trailers and headed out of the compound to gather cattle in the North Adobe pasture: 21,000 acres, 31 square miles of rough, rugged, high desert grazing land. It was home to mountain lions, coyotes, badgers, bobcats, eagles, hawks, and rattlesnakes, as well as to 400 of the ranch's cows, their calves, and forty bulls. This high, remote, isolated pasture, thirteen miles from the head-quarters, was filled with deep ravines carved in the treacherous rocky foothills of the Sierra de Las Uvas Mountains, and gathering cattle in this pasture would test the horsemanship and cattle sense of Pete's roundup crew to the limit.

The cattle the cowboys would be gathering were Brangus and Brangus crossbreds, a Brangus being a mixture of three-eighths Brahman and five-eighths

Angus. This combination was ideal for the climate, altitude, and the rough, harsh topography on the Corralitos. The cattle were good, protective mothers and great foragers. The previous owner, Dorrance Roderick, had developed a breeding operation to establish the Brangus breed on the ranch, to raise and sell breeding stock. But during Pete's tenure the Corralitos didn't have a formal breeding program; such a program required a lot of additional paperwork, along with a constant vigil and secure pasturing for the breeding animals, so it was quite different from a cow-calf operation. Our cow-calf operation was designed to get the ranch calves to gain as much weight on pasture as possible. Then they were shipped to California for fattening in the feed yard, then on to slaughter in the packing house. Cull cows, old bulls, and crippled livestock were also shipped to slaughter. Some of the better heifers—the females with good conformation and sound bone structure—might be saved and kept on the ranch as replacements in the herd.

One hundred fifty bulls of different breeds—Brahman, Santa Gertrudis, Charolois, Simmental, and Brangus—were purchased from other ranches or cattle breeders to improve our cow-calf operation by broadening the gene pool, because the herd gained hybrid vigor by crossbreeding. When purchased, they were young, serviceable adult bulls; whether horned or poled made no differ-ence. When paired with the cows, they produce calves with distinct Brahman characteristics: strong, adaptable, and perfect for the land they would graze for a year. We also grazed steers at times when the pasture was lush, and had forty head of contrary, unpredictable, and dangerous bison pastured and fenced off in the interior of the ranch. But for this roundup the cowboys would be gathering a large cow-calf herd in the rugged North Adobe, a troublesome, difficult pasture. Roundup that morning was the main attraction on the ranch, and the cowboy crew had all of Pete's attention.

The biggest obstacles in gathering the North Adobe pasture were the Uvas Mountains to the north and west, and the Rough and Ready Hills to the east. The isolated pasture was filled with deep ravines and drop offs, and the high rock faces at the base of the mountains, which formed much of the northern boundary of the ranch, were a natural barrier to the cattle. This stretch of no-man's-land up against the mountains had gaps in the rough and tumbled fence line caused by landslides of shard rock that cracked off the canyon cliff faces, slid down on the line, tore it through, and sometimes completely covered up stretches of it. This fence line and ranch boundary traversed ten miles along the base of the mountains and was accessible only on horseback or by foot except for one road running north and south, which split the pasture in half. This road was used to trailer the horses and riders to the fence line in the northern extremes of the pasture at the base of Magdelena Peak, where the roundup would begin. Some riders and horses would unload from trailers here at the base of the mountain; a few would ride to the northeast, some would ride south, and some would unload their trailers six miles away at the southwest corner of the pasture and then ride north. The plan was for all riders to ride into the pasture along the fence line and then drop off one rider every half mile or so, who would wait for the other riders to continue on ahead, dropping off riders for another three miles in order to get into position along the perimeter fence. The northbound riders would eventually meet the riders coming from the south and form a semi-circle of riders inside the fence, so they would surround the cattle on the northern side. When all riders were in position, they would begin cleaning out the cattle along the fence line, kicking cows and calves out of the ravines and into the open. They would engage and prod reluctant bulls to start moving, gradually gathering small bunches of cattle together to form a herd. Then when all cattle had been cleared from the fence line and were headed in the right direction, the cowboys in unison would begin their cattle drive to the corrals six miles to the southeast. The primary concerns were not to miss any cattle hidden in the deep canyons and ravines, or to have any cattle already gathered turn back, get behind the riders, and then scatter back into the mountains. Riders were not to be out in front of the cattle but always pushing them from behind, unless there was a specific reason to be out ahead, such as having to open a gate or to turn the herd. But guests were always prompted to stay behind the cattle, while the seasoned cowboys were responsible for any maneuvers on horseback out ahead of the herd.

Veteran cowboys not only had to control the cattle but—like busy babysitters—also had to keep a wary eye on the guests' actions on horseback. The over-eager rookie riders who wanted to prove their horsemanship on a cattle drive were a special problem, for they could disrupt the roundup if they were impatient and didn't follow instructions from the cowboys. Such instructions might be only the warning wave of an arm and a hat from a half-mile away, or a resounding holler or piercing whistle from closer by, signaling a guest to stop what they are doing or stop where they are going and get back behind the cattle. Guests who were out of position or impatient, or who rode in ahead of the herd, might make the herd turn to avoid the rider and split-up; then the herd would have to be regathered, with a loss of precious time and unnecessary stress to the cattle and the riders.

Once the cattle began forming small bunches at the base of the mountains and were heading in the right direction, to the southeast, the riders allowed the cattle to move at their own pace, with cowboys continually gathering singles and bunches of cattle into the herd from all sides of the pasture as the roundup progressed. Responsible guest riders spent considerable time just sitting on their horses, waiting and watching behind them for cowboys who were gathering cattle and pushing them to catch up with the growing herd. The greenhorn riders had to pay attention at all times or they could suddenly be out of place and cause a problem. Guests weren't really necessary to the roundup, and were more or less just along for an exciting ride; but, even so, they had to behave on horseback and pay attention, since their actions or inaction could cause havoc in gathering the herd.

Pete on horseback climbed a high mesa at the back of the pasture along the northern fence line and paused at the top to catch a bird's-eye view of the roundup going on below. From his high vantage point in the rocky foothills overlooking the vast pasture, Pete could watch the movement of cattle gathering together from miles apart and slowly pushing to the southeast toward the corrals. Then he saw Leonard, the ranch foreman, and another rider a half mile away cleaning cattle out of a deep canyon, the red dust whirling around the riders and cattle as the cattle on a high trot streamed out of the canyon with the cowboys in pursuit. But an old bull in the bunch suddenly turned back, refused to move ahead, wanted to fight the cowboys, and blocked the narrow canyon. He was spinning around, pawing the dirt, charging the riders, causing quite a commotion in the bunch, and as a result about thirty stirred-up cows and calves ahead of the bull were scampering out of the open end of the canyon at a high trot. The fracas with the bull had split the cowboys from their cattle, and the animals were now scattering in different directions from the mouth of the canyon, some turning back and hightailing it into the hills. The cowboys couldn't drive the enraged bull any further out of the channel canyon, but the bigger problem now was that the cattle out ahead of the riders were getting away, heading back, and that problem had to be dealt with quickly. Sensing the runaway cows up ahead, the two cowboys at once quit the disruptive bull and scrambled precariously up and out the sides of the canyon. The men split up, heading in different directions along the base of the mountains; they stood in their stirrups, riding guardedly at a trot on the dangerous, steep terrain, but doggedly trying to head off the straying cattle before they escaped back into the hills. Pete intently watched the action below him. At any time he could have ridden off his perch on the mesa to help Leonard regather the cattle, but there was no need because other riders from both sides had seen the cattle break away and had already joined in the effort by circling around and above the cattle before they had a chance to flee back into the hills. So now four experienced riders were spread out above the cattle on the mountainside, blocking their retreat. The advancing cows and calves stopped momentarily. The cows stared intently at the towering cowboys dug in on the hillside. Then, sensing their loss of control of the situation, they turned around, calmly gathered up their calves, and trotted back down the hillside with the riders falling in behind them at a walk.

With the cattle together again, the riders began pushing the bunch toward the southeast to join the larger herd. Pete was delighted with the outcome of the bull fracas in the canyon. It demonstrated the proper way to control cattle, with riders helping other riders, and it proved once again that in controlling livestock, size matters, numbers count, and teamwork is imperative. There was no yelling, shouting, waving, or hesitation. Every rider knew where he should be going and what to do when he got there, the result of years of experience on horseback. Every good cowhand knew the most important things he could do were to always turn back to help other riders, to have patience, especially with the greenhorns, and to stay close behind the cattle, even if he had to eat dust. The disruptive, herd-busting bull in the canyon would be dealt with in due time, but for now the job was to gather up 400 head of cattle and push on to the Adobe corrals.

The majority of the cattle, 300 head, were now gathering in a large flat two miles west of the corrals. A smaller bunch would be brought in separately from the northeast, traversing two difficult canyons and needing six riders sweeping down from that direction to scour the ravines, kick out cattle in the rough, windswept highlands, and then head them south to the corrals. A few of the cattle might intentionally be left back—those cows with baby calves still nursing, because the calf would be too young to wean and unable to keep up with the herd; or any cow who fought the drive and continually turned back from the herd, bawling for her calf and wanting to go back, no doubt to pick up her baby calf from where they were separated by the drive. The calf would now be lying still, hidden in the pasture and awaiting the cow's return. If let back, the cow with her unerring senses of smell and direction would find her calf, even if the calf were left many miles back; sometimes such a pair will follow far behind the herd and eventually end up at the corrals. Aggressive, high headed, on-the-fight bulls might be turned back if they disrupted the flow of the herd, or charged and challenged horseback riders, causing cattle to scatter. Such a mean, dangerous animal would be dealt with later, but for now you left him back and kept gathering the herd as calmly as possible and heading to the corrals. It was better to let one animal go back than to disrupt and jeopardize the entire herd, but there were no hard-and-fast roundup rules in making choices like these on horseback, only snap decisions of experienced cowboys with keen eyes and seasoned reflexes enhanced by years of hands-on encounters with cattle. Every situation was different on a cattle drive. Every animal, ravine, and route was new, determined by the cattle dispersion, forage conditions and the ever-changing gully-washed landscape. But for now there were no glitches and no cattle trying to go back. The two herds were pushing to the southeast and the south and would soon unite at the corrals.

It was quiet at the Adobe corrals, but in the distance could be heard the bawling of calves and the bellowing of cows, the animals now thoroughly mixed up and trying to locate each other as they gathered and approached the corrals. To lure the cattle into the corrals, flakes of fresh hay had been pitched in the two large fenced holding pens adjacent to the chute working areas. The animals would be thirsty after a long drive, so all the troughs were full of fresh water, and proper gates were opened or closed to receive the cattle. When the cattle were entering the corrals it would be necessary for ranch hands around the corrals to get out of the way and stay hidden as much as possible—invisible and silent to the gathering herd as it neared the corrals. With too much human commotion the cattle would spook or turn back from the gates, and anyone talking or sitting on the fence rails could cause havoc corralling the herd. When the cowboys arrived with the herd at the corrals, they would do the hard work on horseback—the dusty bunching, careful pushing and funneling of the cattle into the corrals, while all the ranch hands, guests, and onlookers would be quiet and out of sight.

The two herds converged at the corrals at the same time, with cattle trickling in slowly at first: a cow and calf, then pairs and small bunches. Then the two herds formed a larger herd, gathered at the gates, and began funneling into the holding pens. The cowboys surrounded the herd from three sides, very slowly advancing the cattle forward in a constant, smooth, compacting stream. The horses moved from side to side, sidling with controlled steps behind the herd, sweeping the cattle in front of them, and ready with short bursts of speed to stop any cows from turning back. The horses' attention was glued to the cattle directly in front of them as they compacted the herd nearing the gates; the horses were trained to hold the cattle from turning back with very little reining or spurring by the riders, and often a horse would nudge a slow cow with his nose or lay back his ears, bare his teeth and bite a slow cow on the rump to get her attention, prod her along, and keep the cattle flowing into the corrals. The seasoned cowboys on horseback became one with their horses, forming a large obstacle that posed a formidable, threatening presence to the cattle, and there was fluidity and unison in their moves as the cowboys slapped their ropes on their chaps, drove the last of the herd into the pens, and closed the gates. The twenty-one cowboys and guest riders had gathered 400 head of cows and their calves, and thirty bulls were now settling in the pens. All the riders had made it back to the corrals without serious incident and were watering their horses, then haltering them inside the corrals. The cowboys were happy and relieved for the successful gathering, and the guests were exhausted but exhilarated by their cattle drive. The bawling and bellowing of the cattle was deafening in the pens. The invigorating earthy smells of churned-up corrals, trail dust, and sweaty horses heralded the completion of a successful roundup in the rugged North Adobe pasture. And while the cattle watered, calmed down, and the dust settled, there was time for the cowboys to take a break and eat lunch.

Barbara and Blanche brought lunch to the corrals from the headquarters in a pickup, and several guests from the headquarters tagged along in another pickup to eat lunch with the cowboys and watch the action at the corrals. The ladies parked the pickups and quickly let down the tailgates, dragging out boxes and ice chests loaded with succulent roast beef sandwiches, hot ranch beans, zesty cole slaw, mounds of potato salad, freshly made corn tortillas, cold canned drinks, and thermoses of hot coffee and iced tea. The chuck-wagon crew began doling out large portions of the delicious food to the hungry, ruddy-faced guests who were now stretching their trembling legs, rubbing sore spots, and regaining their footing after six long, demanding hours in the saddle. The tired, happy riders eagerly gobbled up the food, talking, sometimes raving about their experience on the ride. It was a great lunch. There was a sense of satisfaction and relief in the roundup crew, and the cowboys chatted with the guests, critiqued their performance on the ride, and gave them helpful hints to remember for the next cattle drive. The gathering in the North Adobe was successful, but more hard work was yet to come, and as the guests finished eating, the cowboys were remounting their horses to go back to work. It was lunch on the run, and daylight hours were wasting away.

The cowboys on horseback regathered the cattle resting in the holding pens and pushed them into the alleyways to begin processing the cattle and separating the cows, calves, and bulls. The guests would assist with footwork on the ground, running errands, opening and closing gates, and pushing cattle into trailers, but the work on horseback in the corrals required the skills of the cowboy to maneuver and separate the cows and bulls from the calves in the narrow alleyways. Working with the large, sometimes aggressive livestock in the narrow alleyways, cowboys would deftly cut the cows and bulls away from the calves and push them down the alley and through different gates where the cows and bulls would be separated and held for future processing. The calves would be pushed to the loading pens and await stock trailers that would haul them to the headquarters. It was dangerous, dirty, dust-sucking work with many large animals in a confined area, and the cowboys wanted to process the cattle as calmly as possible to avoid stirring up the corrals and creating a miasma of thick dust. On a hot day even a slight breeze was a blessing to help clear the air, and some of the cowboys had drawn up their bandanas as face masks to block the choking dust. Fifty animals at a time were gathered into the alleyway where they were inspected for injury or disability. The cows were visually inspected by looking at their udders to see if they were pregnant: a "dry" cow had a small udder or "bag" and was probably not pregnant. The pregnant cows had larger "bags" in various stages of milk production. The dry cows would be shipped to the headquarters to be pregnancy checked. The pregnant cows in good condition would be left in the corrals, soon to return to the range, a few with baby calves at their side too young to wean. Three pickups pulling twenty-foot gooseneck trailers would singly back into a loading chute, and cowboys on horseback and on foot would push, prod, and lightly compact the calves into the trailers and lock the gates. The pickups would begin the ten-mile haul to unload the calves at the headquarters corrals, then return to the North Adobe for another load. Prior to returning the cows to the pasture, or hauling and unloading them at the headquarters, the cows and bulls would be run into a narrow alleyway and sprayed for insects and internal parasites using a portable spray rig towed behind a pickup. This greatly reduced the stress on the cattle, since during many round-ups the animals were covered with flies, and drenching the cattle with a power sprayer eliminated these troublesome pests. It was a great, immediate relief to the dusty, fly-infested cattle, and the cows and bulls enjoyed the spraying—a cool, inviting respite in a hostile environment. The bulls also would be hauled to the headquarters, to be pastured close by and fed hay and supplement daily during the winter to fit them for the main breeding season during the spring when once again they would be put out with the cows. The bulls were not as good foragers as the cows, and feeding them during the winter was necessary to keep them in top condition, especially during dry spells when a dearth of forage and winter grasses could be expected. The animals were unloaded at the headquarters and the bulls, cows, and calves were separated in different pens and holding areas where fresh hay and water were available. In the next few days the cows would be pregnancy checked, the bulls examined for infirmities, and unsound animals or old cows not pregnant would be culled. The calves would be processed, branded and loaded into semis pulling livestock trailers, which would immediately begin the 555-mile trip to the feedlot in California to unload the calves for further processing and placement in the fattening pens. Timing and coordination were imperative; it was vitally important to ship the animals to the feed yard as quickly as possible to avoid sickness and stress to the calves. Prior to shipment, a physical inspection of the branded calves and their shipping papers would be necessary, and all documentation pertaining to the shipment would be examined by the state livestock inspector for final approval. This arduous, continual process of gathering and shipping would continue daily throughout the roundup until all the cattle were put back out to pasture, shipped, culled, or penned for future processing. Back at the Adobe corrals, Pete was finishing the spraying of the animals and the loading of the calves, which might take several hours. But the ranch hand who tended the outside water lines drove into the corrals and gave busy Pete some information he was happy to hear.

The water boy told Pete he had seen the problem bull that was creating havoc in the canyon; it was walking out of the canyon and onto the flatlands heading for water, and Pete knew it was his chance to capture the disruptive bull and haul him to the headquarters. Pete hollered at me to bridle two horses that were haltered in the corrals, and to get Roberto Pacheco, Howard's top cowboy, who was already on horseback in the corrals, to help us gather the bull. We loaded three horses in the trailer and headed north out of the corrals on a rutted, rocky, water-line road heading back into the foothills. As we came over a rise in the road, we spotted the old bull slowly walking towards a distant water drinker, unconcerned at our presence. I stopped the pickup. Pacheco got out, unloaded and mounted his horse, and slowly walked towards the bull as it plodded away on a beeline toward the drinker. Pacheco took loose his long rope from the side of the saddle, and in a circular motion, with his right hand inside a coil, began shaping a five-foot noose at the end of the rope. He didn't want to rope the bull, and would much prefer to drive him a mile and a half back to the corrals and load him calmly into a trailer through a chute. Roping any animal in open range is stressful to the animal and dangerous to the cowboy, who must have a definite plan as to what he's going to do with the animal once it is roped. Pacheco's roping venue was not in a flat sand-filled arena with grandstands, but brushy, hard, holey, untouched terrain where the ground was pockmarked with pitfalls that could easily stumble a horse, and there were expanses of tall brush and large patches of prickly pear and bayonet cactus with two-foot blades and three-inch spines that could stick and impale any animal. A rope thrown from a horse could snag in the brush and cactus, entangling the cowboy and his horse in the coils of the rope and killing or injuring both, and such accidents can happen in a split second working with cattle, especially when roping them. It is dangerous business. Pacheco would do what was best for the health of the bull even if it meant herding him for two hours, but now the animal must either walk to the corrals with Pacheco pushing him, or the bull would end up exhausted but alive, and locked in the front of the trailer heading towards the headquarters. An ornery, man-attacking bull would not be abided on the ranch.

As Pacheco neared the bull, his mare began flaring her nostrils, snorting and wafting the air. She had her ears cocked forward and her eyes locked on the bull, who had spun around forty feet ahead of them and now had his head down, pawing the ground with one hoof then the other, glaring up at the cowboy with fierce red eyes from a cloud of dust. It was time for the showdown. Would the bull charge or retreat? Pacheco, with his rope held high at his side, inched the horse slowly towards the bull, now thirty feet away and facing him on flat ground. Then with one last pawing of the dirt, the bull exploded in a head-on charge at the horse and rider. An instant before the bull could savagely butt the horse, Pacheco, with the coils of his rope and the reins clenched in his left hand and his loop in his right, reined his horse sharply to the right and spurred her so she bolted sideways out of the bull's path. At the instant the bull passed by the horse's side, within inches of her rear flank, the mare spun in a tight half circle to the left on her back legs and landed on four hooves behind the bull as he charged by. With two quick twirls of the loop at his side, Pacheco threw out his rope, almost underhanded, in a long loop that slapped up under the bull's belly and fell to the ground. The bull's right rear hoof landed in the loop, and Pacheco drew back his arm and with a flick of his wrist to cinch the loop securely on the animal's leg just above the hock. Then he played out thirty feet of rope as the animal charged by in a rage, dragging the rope with his right leg. The bull—having missed his target on his first attack and now roped on his right rear hock—again spun around and stopped, further enraged, and ready to mount another charge at the horse thirty feet away and facing him again. Had Pacheco roped the bull around the neck, the bull would be able to charge him continually until Pacheco finally would have to choke the animal into exhaustion in order to subdue it. If he had roped him by a front leg the animal could still charge forward and attack the mare and rider with his vicious front hooves, and Pacheco would need to be in constant retreat until the bull was exhausted, laid down and refused to go any further. This treatment could render the bull unable to move again or even kill the aging animal, but this wouldn't happen because the wise Pacheco had roped the bull on one rear leg.

Pacheco coiled back the slack in his rope and wrapped it twice around the saddle horn. The rope tightened in a straight, taut line between the horse and the enraged bull, who was now furiously pawing the dirt and sending dust and rocks flying in the air behind him. Then like a sprinter exploding from the starting blocks, the bull charged again. But Pacheco reined and spurred the mare to the left three feet and tightened the rope on the saddle horn, jerking the bull's right rear leg forward and pulling his rear end around. This threw the animal off balance in mid-charge and crashed him to the ground twenty feet in front of Pacheco. The bull regained his footing as Pacheco coiled up his slack and rewrapped the rope on the saddle horn, again tightening the rope on the bull's leg and waiting for the next move. Instantly the bull charged, and again Pacheco, with his horse and rope, jerked the bull's back leg forward, to throw the bull sideways and off balance in his charge. The animal stumbled and then tumbled to the earth, landing hard and sending a thick plume of dust into the air. The old bull slowly rose onto four legs, his anger now turning to fear; he was thinking of retreat, and he threw his head from side to side looking for an escape from the horse and rider. Then in a burst of speed he charged left, away from the formidable cowboy, and headed toward the southeast, in the direction of the Adobe corrals. Pacheco fell in behind him stride for stride, the bull dragging the rope with the loop end still cinched on his rear leg, the other end secure in Pacheco's grip, ready to wrap again on the saddle horn if necessary to control the critter. The cowboy and bull were now in a high trot. They sped toward the corrals two miles away, busting brush and cracking through the undergrowth as they snaked their way through the ravines and cactus at a fast, dangerous gait.

Pacheco, in a high trot right behind the bull, switched his rope from side to side over the mare's head as the bull tore through the brush, jumping low spots, and cutting right and left as he tried to evade the determined cowboy close behind. Both still headed rapidly toward the distant corrals. Pacheco hoped the old bull would slow to a walk to save his strength, but the animal pressed on, trotting faster as it tried to reach the sanctuary of the corrals and shake off his relentless pursuer. Pacheco patiently paced the mare from side to side, gently reining her back and forth, sweeping behind the bull, keeping his rope high and free from the brush. The cowboy's eyes were glued to the bull and the ground, watching carefully for holes and snags in the rugged terrain that could stumble the mare or entangle his rope. As the bull neared a ravine, he slowed to a stop, then gathered himself and sprang forward in a leap, trying to cross the ravine. But now weary, he missed his jump, slid back off the sides of the ravine and came to rest on his belly in the sandy bottom with his legs under him. He didn't try to get up again. The tired old bull could move no further. He had quit, and no amount of prodding, whipping or poking would prompt the exhausted, sullen critter to move another inch, at least not until he had rested. But if the blood supply was cut off to his legs for too long, and his legs "went to sleep" in this down position, the stressed old bull might be too weak and unable to rise on his own again. Pacheco waved his hat from a distance, signaling us to bring the trailer and horses and back the trailer in as close as possible to the bull, now curled up in the sand.

Pete and I, in the pickup pulling the trailer, left the road and maneuvered through the brush and rocky terrain, winding through the stumps and cactus, trying to keep an eye on the action and get close to Pacheco and the bull as fast as possible. Pacheco had driven the bull out from the hills and onto flatter ground, knowing that if the bull went down, we would have to get the trailer in close with in order to load him. In a deep ravine, where you could not get the trailer close, the bull might be impossible to remove without injuring him. Fortunately this ravine was small and accessible enough in the rough terrain to back the trailer into a position where, if necessary, the 1,200-pound bull could be dragged into the trailer using horses and ropes. We stopped the pickup away from the bull and unloaded our horses, then opened the front compartment of the trailer and swung open the rear gates where the bull could enter. Pete mounted his horse and held the reins to my horse. I backed the trailer up the ravine toward the downed bull and stopped just short of the subdued animal, now resting only four feet away from the open trailer gates. We were ready, if necessary to use a hot-shot—a hand-held shocking device—on the bull to get him to stand up and move him enough to load him in the trailer. Also, both Pete and I were ready to rope him around the neck, then run our ropes inside the trailer through to the front compartment, pull the ropes back through to the outside of the trailer at the front compartment, rewrap the ropes on our saddle horns, and, with the horses on opposite sides of the trailer, drag the bull into the trailer's front compartment head first. But further roping or dragging would put additional stress on the old animal, and luckily, today, this rough treatment wasn't necessary to load the ornery, worn-out bull.

As I parked the pickup and jumped out to mount my horse, the old bull—seeking a respite from the onslaught of the cowboys—picked himself up off the ground and stood for a second; then without prodding, whipping, or shocking with the hot shot, he took two steps and jumped up into the back of the trailer, then slowly walked to the front compartment and stood quietly. Pete, from his horse, reached into the trailer and slammed shut the gate on the bull. Then Pacheco, with a flick of his wrist, snapped free the noose from the bull's hock, recoiled his rope and lashed it to his saddle. The bull, having been hauled several times before, sensed the sanctuary of the trailer. It was his port in the storm, a refuge from the constant confrontation with the relentless, overwhelming cowboys, and he now stood silently, subdued in the front of the trailer, uninjured, and ready to be hauled to the headquarters for further processing. A few weeks of fresh hay and water would fit him up before he went on to the slaughter house in Deming for sale. There was a sense of relief that the gathering of the bull ended so easily and without further complications, and with the exception of a few scratches, not a man or animal was injured. But the bull gathering was nothing more than part of a day's work, another ranch job accomplished. Aside from a few nods and satisfied grins, nothing needed to be said about capturing the wayward bull, or Pacheco's amazing display of horsemanship, roping skills, and professional cow sense. Of cowboys, Pacheco was the best of the best.

We loaded our horses in the back compartment behind the bull and headed out of the rugged pasture to the main road, where we met the last of the roundup crew leaving the Adobe corrals and heading for the headquarters in pickups and trucks pulling trailers loaded with cattle and horses. The cabs were stuffed with veteran cowboys and ruddy-faced, worn-out, but happy guests, some sipping beers, all heading to the headquarters for a probable cocktail, a delicious supper, and a much-needed night's rest. They would sleep soundly, imbued with fantastic cowboy dreams. Early in the morning, the cookhouse bell would clang loudly, the dreaming would end, and the roundup would start over: the gathering, processing, sorting, weighing, hauling, and inspecting, with all the work necessarily compressed into as short a time as possible. The same cowboy tasks would be repeated day after day for another four days or until the roundup was over. And at that time, the guests would have been totally immersed in, completely sated with, and thoroughly enrapt by the hands-on roundup on the Corralitos, a working ranch experience none would ever forget.

Then it was time for the guests to leave, and slowly they would pack their things, load their horses and gear, and, vehicle by vehicle, trickle out of the ranch, wistfully looking back, heading home. Some would remain a day or two longer and take advantage of the great shopping for authentic southwestern clothing and jewelry. There were fantastic bargains. The lowest-priced and highest-quality turquoise and silver could be purchased in the shops and boutiques in Mesilla; Barbara and Sally knew the best shops and knew the shop owners personally, so they could always get the best deals. They would patiently see that everyone who wanted to shop could experience and enjoy a trip to town, or two trips. None of the guests would ever forget the hospitality shown to them during their stay, nor forget their hands-on, action-packed horseback experience. Eventually all the guests would go home, but before they left everyone would thank the Corralitos crew for their kindness and attention, and beg to come back to roundup the next year.

***

The morning of the first day of roundup, I was on horseback helping to gather the eastern third of the Adobe pasture, the highest, most rugged and hostile pasture on the ranch, while Lawrence and other cowboys were gathering cattle in the same pasture somewhere to the west of me. I had ridden out to a corner in the far north end of the pasture, and finding no cattle, I worked back and forth, east and west, scouring the ravines and heading southward toward the corrals four miles away. It was a dry run for me that morning; I hadn't seen or gathered any cattle along the rocky, desolate northern fence line, and I felt remiss in my job of gathering, since I was riding toward the corrals without pushing a single cow. But it was a crisp, cool, still morning, and the pure air and twenty-mile vistas from the high plateau pasture were exhilarating.

I stopped on a high ridge overlooking two deep canyons to my east and to my west, and I turned around in my saddle to look for anything behind me, riders or cattle kicking up dust. There, deep in the Silva Canyon to my west, was Lawrence, alone in the canyon, sitting erect on his mule and riding easily in the saddle, with a red bandana knotted around his neck and his hat pulled down to shade his eyes. He was pushing thirty cows and their calves out ahead of him, the bunch slowly snaking their way south toward the corrals, walking at a controlled pace on a cow path at the bottom of the canyon. He had done an amazing job of gathering the cattle in the high, treacherous canyon, especially alone and considering his age and physical limitations, but there was Lawrence at his best: my boss, my benefactor and my antagonist, doing a remarkable job of gathering cattle in the desolate, remote pasture. He was able at some point in his ride to get behind the cattle deep in the canyon; his access was greatly hindered by steep slopes, sheer rock faces, and outcrops of cracking red granite boulders punching through the earth and dotting the hostile high terrain. I marveled at Lawrence's mastery in controlling the long, stringy bunch of cattle in front of him; they stretched for an eighth of a mile and formed a sinuous, dusty, black line streaming out of the canyon. It's a difficult way to herd cattle for any cowboy, having to control them from behind. His cowboy skills impressed me, especially when I hadn't gathered or even seen any cattle the whole morning.

As I was high on the ridge above Lawrence and watching him gather his cattle, I mused how wonderful it would be if he could manage to gather the people surrounding him in life as easily and quietly and mercifully as he handled the cattle lined out neatly in front of him. He was so capable, caring, and sensible handling cattle; why couldn't he just gather his family and friends the same way, with caring, understanding, and loving for the wonderful people who wanted to love him and share their lives with him? Well, the answer was that there was never an accounting for Lawrence's antics. He answered to no one, and the result was he could get away with his instantaneous outbursts and caustic verbal dress-ings-down of people, abuse that caused so much ill will and hurt. An ordinary man for such actions would suffer severe consequences. I still wanted at times to kick Lawrence in the shins for his rude, belittling treatment of people, especially his treatment of Bertha, as well as his alienation of his son, George. But this morning as I watched his skilled horsemanship and admired his cow sense. I tried to forgive, love and respect him in spite of himself.

And I thought of Pete's beneficial influence with Lawrence, and I was happy and thankful because all of us in the family had profited from Pete's benign but profound effect in keeping Lawrence straightened out. Pete many times intervened for family members or friends whom Lawrence had lambasted or demeaned without cause, and I was very happy to have Dad as a buffer between Lawrence and me, because as much as I might disagree with Lawrence's behav-ior, I could never disrespect him. Many times during his outbursts of cursing, ranting, and treating people poorly, I wanted to get in his face and confront him, but that was not prudent—and thanks to Pete's presence, not necessary. Dad was my lighthouse, my harborage, and my anchor during stormy times in my life abiding Lawrence. So, straddling my horse and staring down at Lawrence from my perch on the high ridge, I realized it was time for me to stop musing and get to work gathering cattle. Nothing was worse for a cowboy's reputation than to return to the corrals empty-handed, so I reined my horse off to the east into the steep, craggy Coyote Canyon, and slowly descended its devilish slopes, seeking a big bunch of cattle to gather as retribution for not having found any earlier. And on this beautiful morning during roundup, Lawrence and I would happily ride out our separate canyons leading to the corrals, both doing what we loved to do.

5

Buffalo

Pete loved tending livestock, but he also loved developing water resources and growing crops. When Pete and Sally first arrived at the ranch, his first large project not involving cattle was developing irrigable acreage and sinking additional wells to pump groundwater water out of the basin around the headquarters. There was a substantial water reservoir in this basin, and Pete intended to determine the size of the reservoir, locate the best spots to drill wells, and eventually pump underground water onto irrigated fields. He would farm alfalfa, grow lush winter wheat pasture and a wide assortment of vegetables. With enough water, the rich, untouched, sandy loam soil would produce bountiful yields of a variety of crops. Pete had to determine the maximum acreage that could be irrigated from the underground basin and the amount of water necessary to produce crops or pasture. This basic knowledge and documentation of his land use, along with the actual irrigation of the acreage on a consistent basis, would be important years later when the state of New Mexico would adjudicate water rights. Adjudicating water rights meant establishing ownership of the acre-feet of water underground claimed by the landowner who had put the water to beneficial use. It was very important to find out the size of the underground basin, its depth, and the drilling locations most likely to produce a large volume of water. Howard and Lawrence were fully behind Pete's efforts to develop this most valuable resource, precious water, and put it to use, and Pete was thrilled to have this farming project. He was in his heyday.

Early one morning at the beginning of Pete's water project, as I was driving out of the headquarters and heading up the road, I noticed Pete out of his pickup in the pasture and walking to and fro, alone, about a hundred yards away. This looked odd, and I pulled off into the pasture and drove toward him to see what he was doing. As I neared him, it appeared he was doing some sort of dance on the hard sand. He was slightly hunched over, moving around inside a circle about twenty feet across, and had both hands out in front of him, shuffling his feet back and forth across on the rocky soil. He moved like a man trying to feel his way in the dark; he backed up and turned, made a series of quick steps and then suddenly stopped, with both arms, pointed downward toward the ground. I pulled up and got out of my pickup. I could see Pete concentrating, staring down at the ground with a forked stick clasped in both hands. With the end of the stick he marked an X on the ground in front of him, and then I knew what he was doing and why he was acting strangely. Pete was witching a well—he was searching for water. He told me to gather some rocks and make a marker on the X, because that was the spot where he intended to drill his first new water well. Pete had already been very successful at witching wells elsewhere, and I wasn't going to dispute his prowess of finding underground water with a forked stick, but still, I was skeptical. Nevertheless, I started gathering big rocks and piling them up on Pete's chosen site, and a jubilant Pete jumped in his pickup and drove directly to the headquarters to call the well driller.

Water witching had been used for centuries to find underground sources of water. No one understood how witching worked, if it worked at all. Many believed it was just lucky when a person could find water using a stick. Pete's witching tool was a three-foot-long forked willow branch stripped of its leaves, and when he witched his wells he was totally involved in the process. Earlier he had determined from the lay of the land, the elevation, and the drainage where water might be found, and his witching stick would mark the final spot to sink the well. His method of witching was to hold the forked end of the stick with both hands palms up, very lightly, gingerly, using his fingers and thumbs to balance the stick out in front of him, trying to get as much action from the stick as possible. Then he would amble about in his target area seeking water. Supposedly, the more water beneath you, the more the stick would tend to bend downward, and eventually touch the ground over the highest concentration of underground water. Old timers thought witching was a divination, some sort of a subtle, perceptual force field between the man's hands and the stick that produced results, but no one completely understood it, and few people could witch a well successfully. I tried it once and I just plodded around the ground, feeling silly and embarrassed. I never even felt a quiver from the witching stick and I never found any water. Dad said you have to believe that it'll work or you won't be able to witch, but that didn't make sense either. Although I was eager to help Pete, I was still unconvinced of any power possessed by the stick, and I just finished piling up the rock marker and went back to work. Six weeks later, the well had been drilled, the electricity connected, and a 100-horsepower submersible pump was installed in the well. When completed, the system could pump 500 gallons per minute of potable water continuously, 24 hours a day. It was the largest pocket of water ever discovered in the Corralitos basin, a pure, abundant source for irrigation or domestic use. Drilling this copious well was the beginning of the farming operations on the Corralitos. It demonstrated Pete's love of water, and his tenacity in finding and perfecting it. It was a great example of his determined, inventive genius.

Drilling the first well began a farming operation that would eventually include seven wells connected to eleven circular sprinklers, which would irrigate 550 acres of winter wheat and alfalfa fields. It was a large project that required leveling the raw, untouched land to form the fields. A bulldozer was used to rip out brush, fill in deep holes, and level the land. The big dozer then pulled a land plane across the rough land to scrape, even out, and smooth the planting surface of the fields, and to slope them properly for drainage. Earthen dikes were pushed up and packed down by the bulldozer around the fields to divert flash floods that could wash down the deep arroyos of the Sleeping Lady Hills and inundate the farming acreage below. A mile and a half of irrigation pipe was laid to furnish water to the sprinklers, and electrical hooks-ups were dropped from the trans-mission lines to power the wells. Sprinklers were added as quickly as Pete could locate reliable sources of water and prepare the fields. Most of the work was done by Pete's crew with the equipment Howard and Lawrence sent to the ranch on numerous semis, and Howard provided top-notch mechanics to service the equipment when necessary. With the irrigation in place, Pete planted alfalfa and winter wheat pastures, and the plentiful water quickly turned the headquarters into an oasis of large verdant circles of forage crops. For several years Pete farmed alfalfa and sold the hay to the dairies in the Mesilla Valley. It was top-quality hay, but required a crew of men and expensive equipment to irrigate and harvest the alfalfa during the six-month growing season. The work was continual, day and night when the crop was in the field, and especially during the monthly harvests of the hay. Each month the alfalfa would have to be cut at a certain growth stage to preserve its quality. A mower would cut the hay and lay it in a windrow behind the mower, where the hay would dry and cure for a day or longer, depending on weather conditions, before it was baled. Occasionally, a rake was pulled behind a tractor to turn the hay for better curing or gather it into a windrow if it had been rained on or ripped apart by scattering wind gusts. This would keep the windrows straight for baling. The hay would normally be baled at night as soon as the dew sat in on and humidified the windrowed hay for proper baling. In the morning, after baling, a loader picked up the bales in the field to be sold to the dairies, and stacked the bales on the ground or loaded them directly on flat- bed semis that hauled the hay to the dairies. The farming work was continual. All hands on the ranch took part in the hay harvest if needed, with cowboys driving hay rakes and yard boys operating mowing machines. Sprinklers ran day and night, and there was a procession of daily tasks where timing was important and everyone was on call.

Baling hay was not only work—it could be a pleasure when the hay was cured and the weather cooperated. I baled hay at night, in the early morning hours when the cooling dew softened the hay so it could be baled without shattering the leaves and losing their vital nutrients. I would rise and be in the field early with the tractor and baler and ready to bale, only waiting on the nighttime cooling of the high desert to produce precious dew. As the dew settled in, the hay lost its brittleness and became pliable, and then it was time to bale. The tractor would tow the motorized baler which would pick up the fresh windrow and pack the loose hay into a 140- pound bale, then spit the bale out the back onto the ground. Baling produced a cadence, a flow of rhythm and a controlled rumbling feeling and sound. The steady drone of the pull tractor and the low roar of the baler's diesel motor blended smoothly together, and the powerful baler engine would growl and grunt as it tightly packed the windrowed hay. The powerful sounds and rhythm of the equipment was satisfying, while the aroma of the freshly cured hay with its sweet, inviting scent of fermentation blended perfectly with the cool night air. All the while, the machine was producing nutritious bales of hay, a bale every nine seconds, and over a hundred tons of hay was baled the entire evening. On cloudless nights, thousands of stars were lit up, each so bright and distinct in the thin mountain air that it seemed to be hanging alone, suspended in the black moonless sky. My baling work was a pleasure, and the sights, sounds and smells were delightful. These productive nights were an enjoyable break from the daily routine of tending cattle and fixing water lines.

Not all farming operations went as smoothly as baling that night, and every day growing crops was filled with glitches and setbacks. Thunderstorms would strike the wells with lightning, sometimes causing extensive damage and normally requiring repair. We had to be constantly vigilant of the sprinkling system, especially during the night; someone was always on call to stop the pumps and shut down irrigation if necessary to prevent flooding the fields and bogging down the sprinklers in the event of electrical failure. Equipment malfunctions were common, and parts had to be brought in from Las Cruces or El Paso, or shipped from California. Pete and his crew of men were constantly repairing old water lines, installing new ones, and maintaining the sprinklers.

Pete eventually put 500 acres under irrigation, and the farming of alfalfa and the grazing of wheat pasture continued throughout his tenure. He had fulfilled the requirement for the water right by irrigating with the water. He had also determined the capacity of the reservoir and knew its limits. He had calculated how many acre-feet of underground water existed and how much the ranch was using on a continual basis. This would translate into millions of gallons of underground water owned by the Corralitos—a very valuable asset in a dry, harsh land. This cultivation and documentation was the crowning achievement in Pete's lifelong quest for water.

***

"American bison" and "American buffalo" are two accepted names for the same beast. It is the largest terrestrial animal native to North America, and a healthy bull can weigh more than 2,500 pounds. Buffalo are nomadic grazers that form maternal herds that can migrate over distances of twenty miles a day in search of forage and water. At one time over sixty million existed on a range from northern Mexico through the United States plains and north into Canada. In their natural habitat, they can sprint at forty miles an hour and can run at a lumbering gallop at 25 miles an hour over rough terrain all day without rest. A buffalo, standing still, can jump six feet vertically into the air. Both male and female are horned and have sharp, hard hooves to paw and strike with. Their short curved horns are sharp and are attached to a massive head used to butt and slash with when fighting off predators or when they are attacking anything trying to intimidate them. In their natural state they are unpredictable killers and will attack without warning. These belligerent animals fear nothing. Early naturalists noted, "Buffalo were dangerous, savage animals that feared no other animal, and in good condition could best any foe," and the cows are especially aggressive when in herds and tending young calves. The majority of attacks and injuries to humans in the National Parks System occur with buffalo, more than bears and all other wild animals combined.

In 1976, Pete, Lawrence, and Howard all agreed it would be an interesting experiment—and perhaps profitable—to graze buffalo on the Corralitos. Lawrence already had a breeding herd of thirty buffalo on his Lucky Five Ranch in California. The herd was growing in size and required more acreage to forage, and Howard and Lawrence decided to try to graze them on the Corralitos. The bosses thought the huge middle and mare pastures containing 21,000 acres in the interior of the ranch would enclose the buffalo and be perfect. The inspection papers were arranged, and the buffalo were shipped to the Corralitos. A four-year-old bull and a five-year-old bull in the herd were in fit condition. The cows were from two to five years old—healthy, and some already pregnant. It was a young, vigorous herd. The buffalo, because of their confinement at the Lucky Five Ranch and lifelong proximity to people, had been somewhat domesticated, and this would help ease the stress of relocating to a new environment. But buffalo can't really be domesticated successfully like the beef breeds of cattle. Cross-breeding beef cattle and buffalo, using artificial insemination, produces offspring called "beefalo," and even they are unpredictable animals that retain part of their wild nature and can't be easily handled. This uncontrollable temperament of the American Buffalo became a daily reality and the bane of Pete and the cowboys who would tend and be responsible for controlling these contrary, wayward animals.

Pete was opening and closing an iron gate on foot when the buffalo from California were unloading. He was using the gate to sort out the buffalo for inspection as the animals descended the loading chute into the corrals, directing the buffalo to one pen or the other. A big bull ran through the open gate, and then in an instant turned around and charged Pete, who was still clutching the swinging gate. The bull, aiming at Pete, butted the gate and rammed it back into Pete, knocking him into the air backwards and crashing him into the split-rail fence. He bounced off the fence and lit on the ground in the alleyway. Several head of buffalo followed the bull, jumping over the top of Pete and pawing the earth as they skirted around him to flee the confinement. They nearly trampled Pete as he lay there; he was still conscious, but badly shaken and disoriented, and it all happened within five seconds. We loaded Pete into the pickup and took him to the hospital in Las Cruces, where he was examined and held overnight. He suffered some lacerations and sore ribs, but luckily, no broken bones, and he guardedly went back to work the next day. The buffalo attack was sudden and Pete was very lucky. The powerful animal butting and ramming the heavy gate could have easily crushed and killed him. This attack on Pete was like the situation of a pedestrian in a crosswalk unexpectedly being hit by a speeding car, and the lesson was clear: When working with buffalo, never take your eyes off them. Buffalo can never be trusted.

The buffalo were released from the corrals into the middle pasture and began adapting to their new surroundings. Mangers were filled with hay for the animals, and the corral gates were opened so they could go back and forth and eat hay for a time to acclimate to the terrain and native forage. But the buffalo left the corrals within a few days and began heading north and foraging through the Middle pasture. Soon they were bedded down at the Big Gap Well, a water tank at the northwestern base of the Sleeping Lady hills six miles from the headquarters. The buffalo loved the earthen tanks. They would wallow in the mud at the edges of the tanks, scooping out slick patches of mud and large swaths of vegetation around the water holes. They would lie on their backs, roll in the mud, and plaster their huge bodies with mud, cooling off and ridding themselves of insects. After wallowing in the thick adobe, they became caked with mud and looked lopsided and prehistoric. The mucky mud that dripped off their bodies, when dried, clung to their shaggy fur and hung down like long brown icicles nearly touching the ground. Pete, however, didn't like the wallowing behavior because it destroyed plant life and could damage the earthen tanks. The buffalo were also destructive to barbed-wire fence lines. They would knock down fences if they were frightened and stampeded, or if they just wanted to graze in another pasture. The animals could trample down a fence, or jump over it, and they frequently jumped over cattle guards, something domestic cattle rarely did. The buffalo were unpredictable in their movements in the two pastures, but as long as they grazed in the middle of the ranch and were surrounded by other pastures, there were no major problems for two years. However as time passed and the buffalo fit themselves to their surroundings, they returned to more of their natural state and roaming was part of that behavior. Pete would need to keep a constant watch on the animals' whereabouts.

The buffalo were loners and never co-mingled with the beef animals on the ranch. They preferred grazing in the isolated spots, walking the fence lines, and investigating the limits of their confinement. The buffalo were usually bedded down in a different location every evening and seldom were seen at the corrals, except to drink. They shunned interaction with humans. The cowboys could control buffalo on horseback only because the buffalo were somewhat domesticated and were accustomed to the cowboys riding through the herd to inspect the animals. The horses were on guard around the buffalo. As the cowboys walked their horses through the herd, the cowponies carefully watched each buffalo. The horses flared their nostrils and took in the smells, twitching their ears and shifting their eyes from buffalo to buffalo, reckoning the disposition of each animal. This fearful appraisal of the buffalo by the horses was an omen of how unpredictable and dangerous the buffalo could be. The water boy would occasionally carry a bale of hay with him on his water route. When he saw the buffalo he would drive out to them and throw out flakes of hay that the herd would eat after he drove away. It was a way of settling the buffalo and getting them used to the human interaction—the sounds and smells of the cowboys and horses, and the movement and proximity of the vehicles. Nonetheless, the buffalo were wary of anything out of their own herd. Visitors to the ranch would want to drive out to the pastures to see the buffalo, and we told them where the animals might be found, but to stay on the main roads. And if they saw any buffalo, only to stop and look at them, stay in the car and never approach the animals. For two years Pete could control the buffalo by grazing them within the two huge interior pastures, but over time the animals would slowly revert to their natural nomadic tendencies, and eventually make Pete's life miserable trying to contain them within the borders of the ranch.

One morning the cowboys on the Lazy E ranch to the west of the Corralitos called Pete and told him they had gathered our buffalo west of the Uvas Mountains in their pasture. The animals had broken down the fence and fled through a high slot canyon that split the mountain and connected both ranches. It had taken their cowboys several hours and some hard riding to gather and push our buffalo out of their pasture, and they were glad to do it once, but they wouldn't be happy doing it again. Pete thanked them and promised them that, indeed, it would not happen again. But within one week Pete received a second phone call: the buffalo had again escaped to the Lazy E and were in the same North pasture where they had grazed before. The buffalo were loose again, and this time we would have to go gather them ourselves. Our neighbor wasn't happy with the trespassing herd. Pete phoned and discussed the problem with Howard and Lawrence, and liability the buffalo had created, and they all decided that they should gather the buffalo and ship them off the ranch as soon as possible. The bosses could no longer abide uncontrollable, wayward animals capable of such destruction on their commercial cattle ranch.

The buffalo were on the move. They had been seen the afternoon before drinking at the Big Gap Well, a tank northwest of the Sleeping Lady Hills, and now, the next morning, they were found in the North pasture of the Lazy E ranch. They had broken down a gate and a section of fence line and traversed nine miles in less than half of a day. Our ranching neighbors were upset, and it was time for us to go retrieve our buffalo.

Leonard and I hooked the trailer on the pickup, saddled and loaded the horses, and with Pete driving, we began the arduous drive west to the Lazy E to gather the buffalo. It was fifteen miles of freeway, then a rough dirt road to travel before arriving at the Lazy E headquarters. At the headquarters we paid our respects and apologized to the management of the ranch, and assured them that the buffalo would no longer be a nuisance, that we were shipping them off of the Corralitos. Leaving the headquarters, we headed north, driving on a bumpy ranch road and crossing stretches of the road that had been washed away by flash floods that had exposed sharp patches of red rocks poking through the rutted, uneven surface. The road was almost impassable with the 16-foot trailer we were pulling, and it took another twenty minutes avoiding the chuckholes to bump and snake along and reach the North pasture. This was the most isolated pasture on the ranch, and this neglected road was the quickest and best approach to get positioned behind the buffalo before starting to gather and push them back onto the Corralitos.

We slowly pulled over a rise and there below in a narrow valley, no larger than a wide arroyo, we spotted the buffalo. They were a quarter of a mile away and a half a mile from the mouth of the slot canyon where they entered the Lazy E. When we stopped to unload the horses, the buffalo heard our noise and caught our scent, and quickly began moving away from us, gathering together and beginning to form a herd in the bottom of the valley. They slid down the rocky slopes, kicking up slag rocks and busting their way through the brush out into a long grassy wash that formed the bottom of the small valley. A bull scurrying down from the hillside wedged his way into the quickening herd, and cows and calves gathered in from all sides. The wayward buffalo were hightailing it eastward towards the mouth of the slot canyon, and leading the herd was the dominant cow—no doubt she was the ringleader of the escape from the Corralitos. She was out in front of the herd making a beeline towards the mouth of the canyon with the rest of the buffalo closing in behind her. There were forty animals, the entire herd, in a line running at a high trot in the rugged bottom, fleeing the cowboys and churning up a stringy cloud of red dust.

Pete waited in the pickup, sizing up the situation, and Leonard and I unloaded and mounted our horses, then headed down slope of the wide arroyo looking to kick out any straggling buffalo in the bottom. There was no need for Pete to mount his horse or for Leonard and me to gather any buffalo. None were left in the valley. The herd had already reached the base of the mountain and were clawing and pawing their way up the sand and crumbling rocks that slid down from the mouth of the canyon. Then the buffalo reached the top and started entering through canyon. One by one, and two by two, the buffalo stuffed themselves into the narrow slot canyon, then spewed out the other side and streaked down the eastern face of the mountain, heading back the same way they came in. The buffalo were gone from the North Pasture in less than fifteen minutes and back on the Corralitos.

The buffalo had us figured out. The moment they heard the pickup clanging and bouncing on the rough road, and caught the scent of the horses, they struck a trail in a hurry back to the security of the Corralitos. Hightailing it was easier for the buffalo than being pushed and harassed by the cowboys. These were swift prairie animals, and outdistancing predators was their specialty. This behavior was also the bane of the buffalo. They were nomadic and migratory in their nature, and this urge to move around continually, was impossible to control on a commercial cattle ranch, even one as large as the Corralitos. The bosses had made the right decision to gather the buffalo and ship them off the ranch.

Our biggest concern was addressed. The buffalo were off the Lazy E and back on the Corralitos, but there was still work to do. Pete turned the pickup and trailer around, and he and his horse headed home. He had a long bumpy ride ahead of him, and he had to get ready to receive the buffalo at the headquarters. Leonard and I rode down into the valley and began scouring through the brush in the bottom looking for straggling buffalo and following the trail of the herd, but as we moved east we found no animals. The herd had fled the valley through the canyon-- they could cross the mountain back and forth at will. Leonard and I would ride out the canyon and fix the fence line on the other side of the mountain, then track the buffalo to where they rested.

We were in no hurry. With all the buffalo out of the pasture and on the run, we weren't going to chase them horseback, and we had fencing work left to do. As we crested the hill, we could see the buffalo trotting and galloping off out in the distance, but we would let them run, then gather them later after they had settled down, and we had enlisted a few more cowboys. On the other side of the mountain, we rode up on the boundary fence line. It was a jumbled up mess of wire and wood strung out all along the ground and not visible in sections. Landslides of crumbling rock and loose slag had knocked the fence down, covered some of it up, and the buffalo had trampled over it going in and out in their rampage. We got off and tied up our horses, and with fence pliers, a wad of baling wire from the saddlebags, and our hands, we dug up and pulled the posts out of the sand and crusty red ground, restrung and tightened the wires back on the posts, and stood the 100 feet of downed fence line upright again. Then we tightened and adjusted the barbed wire along the length of the fence one more time. The old fence would now contain a domestic herd of cattle just fine, but not buffalo. It would never have to contain buffalo again. The bosses had learned their lesson. The quicker they could get rid of the buffalo, the better it would be.

Leonard and I trailed the fleeing herd back into the South Adobe pasture where they had torn down a gate in their escape from the Corralitos. They were following the exact same path in retreat as they did when the fled the ranch. We stopped and repaired a fence and gate the buffalo had run over, then continued on horseback trailing the beasts, giving our horses their heads in a brisk walk and following the tracks. We rode out the arroyos and topped the ridges riding southeast looking for stragglers, but we never saw the buffalo. Their trail of their stampede was obvious with the churned up hoof prints snaking around the sand hummocks, and following the path of least resistance. They were heading back in the same direction as the Big Gap Well, where they had been seen yesterday before their escape. After four hours of fixing fences and horseback riding we caught sight of the buffalo a half of a mile away. The entire herd was watering and resting again at the Big Gap Well.

Back at the ranch, we told Pete that the buffalo had traversed the eight miles back to the Big Gap Well, and were resting. Pete had anticipated the buffalo might return to that tank since it was there we often hayed them to gentle them down, and it was the critters' favorite tank to wallow in. Pete told the water boy to load hay in his pickup and spread flakes of hay out around the buffalo, not to bother them, just spread the hay and drive away from them. Then he was to drop hay along the four miles of ranch road leading to the headquarters, to lure the buffalo in closer to the corrals. When finished there, he was to fill the corral mangers and drop flakes inside the corrals for further enticement. The idea was to attract the buffalo and corral them, then inspect and load them as easily and incident free as possible.

It was late in the afternoon, and Leonard and I weren't going to move the buffalo any further today. We would let them rest, settle down and await Howard and Pacheco, who would arrive later in the evening from California to help us gather and load the animals. We left the buffalo resting around the tank and rode back to the main ranch road heading to the southeast. Pete met us with the trailer and we loaded our horses and drove the five miles back to the headquarters. It had been a very uneventful but necessary ride for Leonard and me trailing the buffalo back onto the ranch. We didn't gather a single head, but at least we were able to fix the fences and the gates the buffalo had torn down in their wild rampage. The trucks would arrive in two days to load and haul the buffalo back to California, and we would have six cowboys saddled up for the gathering. It was now past five o'clock in the afternoon. We finished our drive to the headquarters and unloaded and stabled our horses. We fed them flakes of fresh hay, and poured a quart of rolled oats in each of their mangers, then we called it a day.

Early in the morning, before dawn, Pete was out in his pickup scouting the buffalo. Some of the animals had left the tank and were following the hay trail on the road leading to the headquarters. They were heading in the right direction. There was just one pass through the Sleeping Lady Hills-- it was the only break in the mountains for five miles, and running through it was the road Pete had baited with hay to attract the buffalo toward the headquarters. If the buffalo followed the road and the hay trail, it would make gathering and herding them through the mountain pass much easier.

We saddled our horses at sunrise, loaded them in trailers, and headed out to gather the buffalo. Most of the animals were still bedded down at the tank, and we parked the trailers out of sight of the buffalo, unloaded and mounted our horses. Three riders headed west and would circle around to the south and get behind the buffalo. Two riders would go south to the eastern slope of the mountain and keep the buffalo from circling back into the hills after they were pushed through the pass. One rider would hold his position, and keep the buffalo from breaking away to the north.

Our main concern was that the buffalo would bolt and run. We were positioning the riders to cut off every possible escape route, and the cowboys were riding slowly, slinking along, and trying to stay hidden and out of sight of the buffalo until they were ready to gather and move the critters. The dominant cow had already seen and smelled the riders and her attention was fixed on the cowboys coming from the south. The other buffalo became restless, peering off in the distance and watching for riders. The only cowboys moving now were the riders approaching the buffalo directly from the south, and the buffalo began looking away to the east toward the pass through the hills. That was exactly where the cowboys wanted them to head. Then the dominant cow threw up her head, walked out of the tank basin, and began trotting in the direction of the mountain pass. The rest of the buffalo gathered in from the basin behind her, and soon the herd formed a wiggling stream of shaggy animals snaking around the sand hummocks and trotting toward the pass. Within minutes the entire herd moved into and through the pass, and was trotting down the road on the other side of the mountain, following the cow and heading in the direction of the corrals. The cowboys spread out behind and to the flanks of the buffalo and kept close enough to them to control and turn the animals if necessary. But the buffalo were not bolting. They were behaving in a predictable manner, and for the moment the riders were relieved and letting the animals move at their own comfortable pace.

The herd was in a trot making a beeline for the corrals five miles distant, and they soon would encounter a fence line that would turn them south and lead them directly to the headquarters and confinement. They would cover the five miles in about an hour, gliding over gullies, ravines, and sandy washes, never breaking stride, looking like a long, fuzzy roller coaster running a track and coursing up and down over the tops and bottoms of the arroyos. The cowboys would contain them at a distance and keep the buffalo from turning back into the hills, and the dominant cow would continue her relentless trot towards the corrals, with the entire herd in tow. The cowboys were happy to be trailing the buffalo, not pushing or being challenged by the critters, but the riders were in a constant trot, sometimes in a gallop keeping up with the herd and trying to ride the flank and stay apace with the buffalo in the rough terrain.

The buffalo reached the shipping pasture fence line and turned south along it heading to the corrals three miles ahead. With the fence on one side of the animals, it was only necessary for the cowboys to gather in behind them and watch for animals turning back or making a break for the hills to the west. The buffalo were moving along without a hitch, and the gathering of the herd could not have been planned any more successfully. There was no need for the cowboys to do more than keep the buffalo heading south. There was no herding or bunching, no confrontation with the buffalo necessary. It was likely the dominant cow had planned her route before she trotted away from the Big Gap Well. She knew there was hay on the road, and she could smell the waft of fresh hay blowing northward from the corral mangers. The cow wanted to eat hay, to eat first, and to eat now, and she was on a determined trot to the corrals with the herd following obediently behind her, their heads down and their hooves churning up the sand.

Within an hour, the herd stormed into the corrals and headed directly to the mangers, butting and wedging out one another for the choicest spots to eat. A few trotted to the drinkers for fresh water. When the buffalo were all inside the corrals, the water boy, who had been hidden and awaiting the animals, slammed the corral gates shut and the buffalo were penned. The cowboys drew up outside the corrals, all of them relieved that the buffalo gathering was so quickly and uneventful. They dismounted, tied up their horses, and began securing the corrals. The buffalo needed to eat, rest, and settle down the remainder of the day and night in the corrals, and the trucks would arrive in the morning to haul them to

California. The animals were secure for the night. They were enclosed in the center of the corrals confined by a six feet high iron pipe fence with the posts laced together with strong cable, and the cowboys had latched and wired shut the heavy gates until morning. The buffalo would not knock this fence down. After penning the buffalo it was still early morning. Pete had not anticipated the gathering going so smoothly and quickly, but he had some extra horseback work out in the pastures for the cowboys that would fill out their afternoon, and they all would help to load the buffalo in the morning. All the bosses were pleased that the gathering went so smoothly.

The trucks arrived during the night and were ready to load the buffalo at daylight. The cowboys had saddled their horses and the State Brand Inspector was there, and they all were busy as the first truck backed into the loading chute. The cowboys mounted their horses and began pushing the buffalo out of the inner corrals into an alleyway leading to the loading chutes where the inspector would examine the brands as the animals loaded into the semis. The first truck loaded without a hitch, the buffalo behaving calmly and loading into the trailers with little prodding or pushing by the cowboys. As the second truck was beginning to load there was a disturbance in the alleyway heading to the loading chute. A young 900-pound dry cow, not wanting to load, turned around in the alleyway, and charged back through the riders—head up, snorting, on the fight, and escaping back into the inner corrals. The cowboys and their horses avoided her charge in the narrow alley, but none took their eyes off the mad cow from that point forward. The entire loading operation stopped instantly to watch the ongoing buffalo spectacle. This raging cow had everybody's attention as she spun around in the center of the corrals, and she was now facing the riders who were trotting their horses into the corral to gather her. She had her head down, shaking it threateningly at the cowboys, with her black eyes aflame and fixed on the closest rider, ready to charge him at any moment.

The riders trotting toward the buffalo pulled up their horses, froze in place, and waited for the cow to make the next move. The standoff ended instantly when the enraged cow bolted through the circle of cowboys and charged back into the alleyway. She trotted halfway down, appraising her situation, and gazing up at the top of the six-foot-high split-rail fence surrounding the alleyway. The enraged cow stopped dead in her tracks. Feeling threatened, she coiled herself and sprang upward, her huge body and back legs clearing the top rail of the fence; her sharp back hooves dug into the rail and splintered it as she uncoiled and sprang from the top of the fence. She alit on her feet out in the holding pen, ten feet from the fence, and she was on the run.

The cow turned and bolted to the corner of the small holding pen, nosing wildly in the corner for a way out. Then, finding no gap in the fence, she butted headlong through a barbed-wire gate leading out onto the county road. In a huff, she spun around on the road and jumped a nine-foot-wide cattle guard protecting the road. Mad and ready to fight anything moving, the cow tore off in a gallop doing at least at thirty, coursing through the shipping pasture to the northeast and raising a trail of dust with nothing stopping her.

This escaped, enraged buffalo cow was a serious problem that demanded immediate attention. Pete left half his crew to finish loading the rest of the buffalo into the trailers. The other half went on a posse, hunting down the crazed buffalo. There was no point chasing the cow on horseback from the corrals. She had too much of a head start, and at the speed she was traveling it would be dangerous work horseback, especially in a huge pasture filled with potholes and ravines. Pacheco and two other cowboys loaded their horses in a trailer and headed north on the county road, stopping at four miles, where they unloaded, mounted up, and headed into the ragged foothills towards Robledo Mountain. They hoped to get ahead of the buffalo and stop it before it escaped the ranch boundaries, or at least get close enough to it to shoot it. One of the riders had a scoped deer rifle on a sling hung around his shoulders, and Pete had given him instructions to shoot the buffalo if he could get a killing shot. Once the buffalo escaped from the headquarters, it lost much of its fear of humans and was too smart, too unpredictable, and too dangerous to try and gather again, especially in the brushy, rough terrain of the foothills. Pete drove immediately to the headquarters and notified the county sheriff's office and the New Mexico State Police of the incident, and gave an approximate location where the buffalo might be spotted if it strayed off the ranch. He told the officers to shoot the buffalo on sight, not to approach it, and not to disturb it if it's at rest. He urged them to take a killing shot if they laid eyes on it and then to make sure it's dead before going near it. Pete told them we didn't care who shoots the animal, or what happens to the valuable meat that might be saved off the carcass. We would sign a bill of sale to anyone who shoots it, and give him the whole dead buffalo. In fact, we'd offer him sincere thanks for his time and effort! Pete made it clear that the buffalo was very dangerous, and if it was seen, it should be shot and killed. Any decision about the carcass could come later. Pete or his crew would shoot the buffalo on sight if they found it, and if they shot it in some remote, inaccessible canyon, they would leave it lie and let the coyotes and buzzards fight over the carcass. Pete had had his fill of buffalo!

The buffalo herd was shipped that morning to the feed yard in California for further disposition. Only the mad cow on the lam was unaccounted for, and Pete was awaiting further updates from the authorities in the valley on the buffalo escape. The cowboys had tracked it seven miles to the northwest through the North Hawkins pasture, where it broke through the fence and escaped the boundaries of the ranch about four miles uphill from the Rio Grande River. Pete was personally concerned about the buffalo because he had been physically attacked by one the critters. He knew how fast and deadly a mad buffalo could be, and he wanted no one else to share a similar fate. But after the buffalo escaped the confines of the ranch, Pete had done all he could do. Now, he could only wait for notification that the animal had been killed, and give out any helpful information if necessary. Pete waited, and waited.

Two days had passed and there had been no reports from the authorities or the public concerning the whereabouts of missing buffalo. Even a police helicopter failed to find the critter. The buffalo cow had vanished, and her disappearance would forever remain a mystery. Perhaps her final resting spot was in a remote ravine or most likely she was shot, field dressed, and cut up and packaged as freezer meat. The families living at the fringes of the Corralitos were very resourceful people, adept at living off the land, and not an edible scrap of the buffalo would be wasted if they harvested the beast. They would even utilize the head and the pelt. Most likely no one would ever hear about the taking of the buffalo, and that was just fine with Pete. Howard and Pacheco left and returned to California, where they would once again contend with the contrary buffalo herd, now penned securely at the feed yard. With the shipment of the buffalo completed, and the threat of the mad cow incident dwindling, Pete would sleep easier, and not be awakened in middle of the night by calls from upset neighbors. In the end, all the bosses agreed, even fooling with the buffalo was a big blunder.

6

Christmas and Family

The distress of the buffalo escapade soon passed, and Christmas time was drawing near. This was Pete and Sally's favorite holiday of the year. It was time for the ingathering of family and friends, a pilgrimage of the kin from all over the country to the ranch to enjoy the celebration. Barbara and I loved Christmas, too. Our children would travel from California and Texas, and we all would be reunited for a few days of love, frolic, and buffoonery in the high desert. This short time was such a change from the daily workload and tedium that accompanied the ranching life. The necessary work of the ranch would continue, but the celebration of the family, a regeneration of our spirit, would take precedent for a precious few days. Family would also travel from New York, Washington State, and Nevada, to join in the Christmas at the ranch. The spare bedrooms would be filled with family and friends, and no one was excluded. If you were with the family, welcome to the Corralitos.

The families would start arriving as early as a week before Christmas. We would shuttle them in the van from the El Paso airport sixty miles away, and the van would be busy, sometimes making two trips a day to pick up the excited, worn-out arrivals. Families were greeted at the gates with great fanfare and hoopla, and sometimes two families arrived at once. There were shouts and hugs, and everyone was yapping. Women were face to face talking a million miles an hour, and men were clasping shoulders and turning in small circles, admiring each other. Everyone was giving everyone else a head-to-toe examination, with special attention given to the kids:

"Wow, look at those new teeth coming in!"

"Oh, how you have grown!"

"Okay, grab your bag and let's head for the van, your horse is waiting for you at the ranch!"

The embracing quickly ended and the family hurriedly grabbed their baggage and hustled out to the parking lot. We loaded the van and struck a trail to the ranch.

The crew was full of anticipation. Returning to the ranch for Christmas, especially for the kids, was a thrilling experience, and on this trip they would all revisit their own private haunts and special places. Every view and direction on the ranch was filled with memories of dozens of secret spots and hideaways. Of course they had their horses, and each kid had his own personal arroyo that he would soon relocate on horseback. There were also old out-buildings and a bunkhouse to explore. The kids in their younger years thought the eighty-year-old adobe buildings housed legions of ghosts and ranch fairies, and the hapless, nosey kids would venture into the aging structures and call forth the spirits in séance. Gretchen, my daughter, had her own personal ghost, Maria, who continued to haunt her for many years, and today the grown kids still have nightmarish recollections of the spooks and goblins they awoke in those crumbly old buildings. These precious memories and many others were about to be relived by everyone. The extended family would take part in this Corralitos Christmas for an adventure-filled few days, and they were all so excited.

The headquarters was filled with activity and buzzing with expectation of the Christmas arrivals. Pete fitted and shod the horses, and his crew spruced up the entire headquarters compound. Sally and Barbara stocked the cold room and pantries with food and drinks, and prepared some succulent dishes and casseroles for the freezer. Barbara decorated the headquarters with artistic flair and the Christmas spirit. The Luke Short back bar was lit up and festooned with holly wreaths and garlands. An aromatic, freshly cut pine tree from the high mountains was trimmed with bright colored balls, yards of tinsel, and quirky hand-made ornaments fashioned by the family. The tree stood in the entrance opposite a warm mesquite fire blazing in the fireplace, and the cozy room with its woody scent was always an enticing gathering place, especially for the early morning revelers and coffee drinkers. Christmas was near; the smell of it was in the air.

Pete could hear the clatter of the cattle guards and the whooping and hollering from the open windows of the van as it pulled into the driveway. Family had arrived. They flooded out of the van and ran to greet the headquarters crew, everybody grabbing and hugging. They needed a quick stop to unload their luggage, and then they were off to the barn or to rest in the bar with refreshments. The headquarters was a hub of activity with everyone heading in his own direction.

Five of the grandkids stowed their baggage, grabbed their spurs, chaps and hats from the locker in the cookhouse, hurried outside and jumped in the back of Pete's pickup heading to the barn. Pete had cowboy work for them to do, and the kids were grinning from ear to ear with the thought of riding their horses and gathering cattle. Under Pete's watchful eye they currycombed and saddled their horses and were ready to ride. Pete would settle the kids on their horses before he turned them loose on the ranch, and his cowboy work would be to gather fifty replacement heifers and change wheat fields. He could have easily just opened the gate and the heifers would move themselves, but Pete wanted to size up the riding skills of the kids and give firm instructions on cowboy behavior before he turned them loose on a 200,000-acre cattle ranch. The rules were simple: they were always to ride in groups of two or three, and walk their horses; a slow gallop was permissible at times, but only when necessary. And never gallop your horse heading back to the barn, because the horse wants to get there fast to eat hay and rest. But you must control him and slow him down to a walk or you will spoil him. A horse that isn't trained to walk quickly and easily without constant restraint by the cowboy never makes a good cowpony. They were never to race their horses, and they were to be back at the barn an hour before dark. If they get lost, they were to just stop, loosen the reins, give the horse his head, and he would walk safely home from anywhere on the ranch. There were no cell phones, no communication whatsoever when they were on horseback, and an accident could easily turn into a tragedy if someone were alone and injured five miles back in the rugged, inaccessible hills. Safety was Pete's concern; the kids must practice safe behaviors on horseback, and he trained them to do it. And he would keep training them, forever. The cowboy grandkids moved the heifers in half an hour, and Pete gave them his last instructions and turned them loose to explore the Sleeping Lady Hills. Pete and I rode back to the barn, unsaddled our horses and returned to the revelry in the headquarters, satisfied that our kids could handle most any situation on horseback.

The holiday celebration was well under way in the headquarters and the back bar. The cowboys had made it back and were spinning yarns about their adventurous horseback ride in the Sleeping Lady Hills. The tree was lit up and the fireplace was ablaze in the corner, warm and inviting. Sally was playing a Christmas carol on the piano, and had a trio singing behind her as backup, sisters Lois and Joy, and my son, Pete—yes, another Pete Foster—were accompanying Sally's noel. Gretchen and Carolyn, my niece, were playing in the finals of the Christmas pool tournament. They had defeated all the other pool sharks, and now the two were locked in a strategic and eagle-eyed final showdown on the felt.

Coffee, cold drinks and cocktails were being served, and the brothers-in-law were sipping beers at the corner of the festooned back bar, palavering with Pete and listening to his story about being butted, knocked down, and stampeded over by a herd of enraged buffalo. The men were both laughing and wincing as Pete related his recent brush with death. Barbara's son Brad, an avid hunter, was admiring the prong-horned antelope heads mounted on the wall above the pool table and salivating at the thought of his mule deer hunt on the ranch next season. The savvy big bucks would test Brad's hunting skills, but mule deer beware: Brad was a worthy stalker of big-game animals with bow or rifle.

There was to be a talent show on the Eve, and nieces Christine and Tracey were huddling near the fire with stepdaughter Julie, discussing their part in the show. Tracey was rehearsing them to perform a Pointer Sisters number during their portion of the upcoming show. Nephew Wes, the oldest of the grandkids, was the director for the men's performance, and the men had assembled in the atrium and begun to rehearse their noel, a rendition of "We Three Kings." There would be ranching neighbors stopping by and family friends driving out from the city to watch the gala production and share a cup of Christmas cheer, and they were always welcome. "Ya'll come!"

The beginning of the fun and festivities filled the headquarters with happiness and an overflowing of yuletide spirit, and there was a cold front approaching from the north, with the possibility of snow tomorrow night, Christmas Eve. The prospects for a beautiful white Christmas were steadily improving. Throughout the day tomorrow, there would be time for riding and ranch exploration before the storm arrived, and everyone would choose a favorite ranch activity and pursue it.

Breakfast was served around 8:00 a.m., late by ranching standards, but allowing the families some extra rest before the explorations began. By 8:30, Pete and I had planned two trips. Dad would take riders horseback to explore the natural caverns and silver mines. They would also ride out to the centuries-old dwelling sites of an early Indian culture that inhabited the land, and then view the Indians' childlike pictographs etched on the tall rock faces in a nearby slot canyon. All these vistas were nestled together, making for an easy horseback ride in a remote mountain area of the East Hawkins pasture. Wes and I would lead a small expedition of grandkids to explore the old homestead dumps and ancient arrow point sites that Pete and I had discovered over the years riding horseback and gathering cattle in the isolated pastures. It would be a surprising trip to uncover untouched artifacts and relics from dwellings and sites that were abandoned hundreds of years earlier.

All old homesteads by necessity had dumps. Staples must come in and trash must go out. The isolated homesteads were abandoned throughout the years for any number of bad reasons: drought, the drying up of water wells, sickness, predation of their herds, and harassment by marauding Indians and banditos. It was in these dumps we dug, poked around, and scavenged in the ground with shovels, hand spades and bare hands, through layers of packed sand and grit to uncover treasures from the past. There were relics like small, unbroken blue medicine bottles, rusted hand-forged spurs, rare pieces of early barbed wire, and colorful glass and bone beads that had broken off from jewelry and were strewn about underground. All of these and more were hidden and unmolested for years underground, and each turn of the shovel could uncover some new small bit of history. As the digging and discovery progressed you could hear the kids chattering and marveling at their finds.

"Oh, my gosh! Oh, my goodness! What is this?" blurted out Julie, on her hands and knees pawing the sand.

"That's a tin fork," prompted Wes, giggling at her. "And I found the spoon right here!" he bragged as he held it up and showed it to the crew.

"Look at this, look at this!" chimed in Tracey as she pulled a rusted three-foot length of old barbed wire from beneath the crusty earth. "I am saving this for Granddaddy's collection," she pronounced as she rolled up the wire and stuck it in her treasure sack.

"Wow, look at this!" Brad shouted out. "It's a .50 caliber lead musket ball! Man, if I only had a musket and some powder, I could go deer hunting right now," and he peered off into the foothills, looking for a big buck. Sister Julie, the animal advocate, suggested to Brad that rather than shooting the deer with the lead ball, he should be a real man and kill the deer by just throwing his precious ball at it, and the entire excavation team agreed and howled together in laughter. Wes had scavenged three old hand-forged nails from the late 1800s for another contribution to the treasure trove, and everyone would find something of interest from out of the past. All the antique discoveries from the dumps would be piled on the back bar and displayed at the headquarters that evening. The dump-digging crew had the dig of their lives, and now it was time for these human packrats to move on to explore a coveted riverbed on the east side of the Sleeping Lady Hills and search for arrow points.

Arrowheads, or arrow points as they are called by collectors, were scattered about the ranch, and they could be found almost anywhere if one searched long and hard enough. But it was illegal to remove them from public lands. This was an impossible law to enforce, and over the years many arrow-point collections that were put together by private owners in and around the Mesilla Valley came from the Corralitos Ranch. Some of these collections were extensive and quite valuable. Pete on horseback came across a dried-up riverbed, also called a wash, south of the headquarters, where under certain conditions arrow points could be more easily found. A stretch of this long, wide wash was located on our deeded property, and there we could dig arrow points all day long and collect as many specimens as we desired. The wash emanated from a ravine eroded from a saddle ridge between two high buttes on the eastern side of the Sleeping Lady Hills. The lay and slope of the saddle was perfect for catching large amounts of rainwater during monsoon inundations, and then releasing it downhill, turning the rainwater into a furious, swiftly flowing flash flood that would rampage down the ravine and spread out in the wash. The wash began at the base of the ravine, then broadened out and ran for two miles to the southeast, and it was after heavy rains that arrow points could be more easily found there. It was a low point in the valley, much like the drain in a sink, and everything churned up by the flash floods in the area, including arrowheads, tended to settle at the lowest point, which extended along the flat, hard bottom of this dry riverbed. In some places along it, pieces of arrowheads, and occasionally an intact one, could be picked up off the hard bottom as easily as picking up a coin on a sidewalk.

I hauled the eager scavengers by pickup to a bend in the riverbed midway along its course, and at once they got out and began scouring the bottom of it for arrowheads.

"Whoa!" hollered out Julie, scratching the surface of the riverbed bed with the toe of her boot. "I think I've found something—come here, come here, and take a look at this!"

We all circled Julie and looked down where her scuffing had exposed the point of a chiseled-looking thin piece of flint sticking out from the crusty sand.

Wes dug up the clump of hard sand ensconcing the flint piece and presented it to Julie on the tip of his shovel for a closer look. Quickly she crumbled off the caked-on sand from the flint, and there in the palm of her hand was a nearly intact arrow point. Only the tip of one bottom point was broken off this otherwise perfectly chiseled arrowhead, and whoops, hollers, and accolades erupted from the entire crew at her big discovery.

"I'm going to give this arrowhead to Brad," Julie promised, "and if Brad misses the big deer when he throws his musket ball at him, he can make an arrow out of this and use it when he tries to shoot his prized buck!" And the crew again laughed heartily in approval and applauded her. Wes found an old brass shell casing of a bullet from the late 1800s, and while not as ancient as the arrowheads, it was still an unusual discovery, since early pioneer gun owners rarely discarded their shell casings. After discharging the bullets they tried to save the casings because they were valuable for reloading. Wes's casing was a great find.

"Hey, you guys, look at this!" summoned Tracey as she peered down at the surface of a flat rock slab sunk in the riverbed. Witnesses gathered around her, and there below lay a small, clean arrow point, loose and resting alone on the slab, like someone had recently placed it there by hand.

"Oh, my word," Wes shouted out, "that arrowhead looks completely intact!" Tracey bent down and picked up the small arrow point with her fingertips, and passed it around for the crew to inspect.

"It's perfect," said Julie.

"Yeah, and so easy to find, just lying right there in plain sight on the top of a rock," approved Brad.

"Leave it to Tracey to get something of value without having to work for it," kidded brother Wes, and everyone guffawed at his quip and continued to dig. This small intact arrowhead was the find of the day and would fit in perfectly with any collection, and Tracey received well-deserved kudos from the crew on her precious discovery. The grandkids returned to the headquarters that afternoon with a sack of rustic, antique souvenirs, and the crew was elated with the day's activities of family fun and unity. Everyone that day would find some little old something in the riverbed to add to the bag of treasures, and years later all would remember and cherish the exciting relic-hunting expedition that Christmas Eve.

Pete and his crew of grandkids were going to explore the East Hawkins pasture on horseback. They hauled their horses five miles north from the headquarters, and unloaded them at the run-down, dilapidated ruins of the Hawkins ranch house. They mounted up. My son, little Pete, rode his spirited Arabian cow pony named "J.J.," and Gretchen, the youngest of the crew, was astride Appie, a gentle old Appaloosa mare. Carolyn, the athlete, was in full control and mounted on Foxy, a beautiful blaze-faced sorrel horse. Christine, the oldest, and also the most vocal, rode a sensible ranch horse named Handlebar; and granddaddy Pete led the crew riding Levi, his favorite cow pony.

The cowboy expedition headed east across a dry lake bottom pocked with deep potholes, too dangerous to cross at any pace faster than a walk. They traversed a treacherous ravine and rode into one of the most inaccessible and scenic mountain areas on the ranch. They stopped first to explore the old silver mines and natural caverns on the west face of the foothills of Robledo Mountain. These foothills formed the northeastern boundary of the ranch and were an ideal location for the camps of early Indians. They contained high bluffs and natural caverns with habitable sites high up off the desert floor. From there it was a good lookout for miles around, and was a perfect perch from which to defend themselves from attackers. The caverns were natural windbreaks from the elements, and their smoke-stained walls indicated fires had been burned there centuries ago for warmth, cooking, and protection from predators. The cliff faces also contained the silver mines of the Rough and Ready miners, which were dug in the mid 1800s. They dug their mines using picks and shovels high up on an escarpment not far from the caverns. The miners were a formidable crew of hardy men, and when they were dug in high up on the escarpment and armed with rifles, they could readily defend themselves from marauding Indians. A couple of their mines extended 200 feet back into the hard metamorphic rock. The silver ore in the mines was soon exhausted, and the miners moved on to better pickings, leaving only the entrances to the mine tunnels pocking the cliff faces as a reminder of the miners' visitation.

The grandkids dismounted at the base of the cliffs. Pete stayed on horseback and held the reins to their horses, and the kids climbed up the gravely slopes to the mine entrances. It was wintertime, and the rattlesnakes hibernating deep underground were no danger to the kids, so Pete felt safe to let them explore. Sally and Barbara had made them hearty meat burritos, wrapped them up in foil, and gave them to the kids to stick in their coat pockets for breakfast later. The kids climbed the crumbling slope to the mines and sat down at the entrances to rest, then wolfed down their burritos and began exploring. Their plodding back and forth between the mines and caverns lasted only thirty minutes, and the kids had seen enough of the rocky mines and caverns. As their exploration came to an end, Pete could see them all standing on the mountainside throwing rocks down the slopes at cactus. Boredom had set in, and they were ready to hit the trail on horseback and continue sightseeing with Granddaddy. It was time to ride.

The riders mounted their horses and headed east around the base of the foothills and entered a narrow canyon with rock faces on both sides extending high into the sky. The brush was thick, with only a cow trail to follow through the tangle, and the riders proceeded in single file back into the narrowing canyon. After a few minutes meandering the trail through the thick mesquite, they came upon a twenty-foot high rock face that had been etched centuries ago by the resident Indians. The crude drawings of simple objects—circles, a stick figure, and a few vertical lines—were all that remained from some historic artist's expression. The paintings were etched into the rock face with the point of a harder rock dipped in a mixture of animal blood and iron oxide. This combination, called hematite, formed an indelible dye that penetrated the stone surface and would stain it for centuries. These pictographs on the rock faces and the smooth depressions in the flat rocks nearby were signs that the early inhabitants had ground their grains, prepared their food, and lived in the region centuries ago. This location was only three miles from the Rio Grande River to the east; indigenous populations in the arid desert always tried to inhabit the livable sites closest to a water source, and this one was perfect. The grandkids dismounted and perused the site on foot, examining the stone depressions and running their hands over the pictographs, trying to figure out why anyone would paint such abstracts. Was there a message intended, a code or map, or were the drawings just graffiti or the work of some pariah or nut? The mystery remains today about what the pictographs represented.

The kids had a fun, interesting morning pawing and peering around in the remains of the archaic Indian dwelling places, but once again they were sated with the rocky landscapes and primitive drawings, and wanted action, more saddle time, and they mounted their horses anxious to ride.

The crew was going to head in two different directions. Gretchen, age seven, was getting tired, and Pete decided to escort on horseback and ride southwest seven miles, back to the headquarters, sightseeing along the way. As they rode away, big sister Christine—in her high, shrill voice—could be heard shrieking commands at Carolyn and little Pete, sounding like a barking seal gathering her pups. She was continually yapping and ordering the other two around on horseback, but neither was listening. Little Pete and Carolyn were younger than Christine, but were more experienced riders than she, both having spent several summers on the ranch riding with the cowboy crew, and exploring some of the pastures from fence line to fence line. They weren't about to listen to the greenhorn, Christine. She was just along for the ride. Pete and Gretchen watched them as they rode away toward the headquarters. The three had a lot of ground to cover, and Christine was still jabbering orders at everyone until the riders were nearly out of sight and she could no longer be heard.

Pete and Gretchen waved a final goodbye to the older kids, then turned their horses and rode three miles back to the trailer. They loaded their horses and drove to the headquarters, with Gretchen falling asleep on the seat of the truck during the short drive back. It had been a long, tiring morning for her, but with a quick nap she would be rested and ready to go. There was still a bunkhouse for her to explore, and a ghost or two for her to arouse!

A stiff north wind was beginning to blow. It was getting colder, and a big change in the weather was coming soon. It would be dark around five o'clock and all the grandkids would be back from their trail-riding and explorations before the sun set, to get ready for the celebration. Pete's expedition was a great family outing, and a memory of Christmas time the grandkids would never forget.

Christmas Eve night had arrived and there was busyness and excitement at the headquarters. Snow had begun falling and was building up outside on the ground. Guests had arrived from the valley and were mingling with the family, chatting and catching up on all the latest events. Women were in the kitchen preparing Christmas Eve dinner: a huge pot of spaghetti, a succulent green salad, and hot cheesy French bread. After a long day filled with many activities, the crew was hungry, and spaghetti was always a family favorite. A few kids had sequestered themselves in different rooms, rehearsing their upcoming musical acts, and Lois sat at the piano practicing her backup in the productions. Others were huddled around the back bar sipping their drinks and listening to Pete's precious recap of today's expedition with the grandkids. His expressions and descriptions of the events during the ride were just as funny as actually being witness to the kids' antics, and the bar crowd eagerly gathered around him, listening to his factual and hilarious account of the grandkids' great horseback adventure.

Wes brought in a gunny sack loaded with relics and discoveries he and his crew had unearthed at the dumps and the arrowhead sites, and he poured them out on the back bar for everyone's approval, especially Pete's. Pete was the ranch's official artifact judge; he was the one to impress, and his decision as to the merit of each discovery was final. Pete quickly turned his attention to the relics scattered out on the bar and began his appraisal. Pawing his way into the pile, Pete first noticed Tracey's specimen of the rusty old barbed wire she had uncovered, and Pete's eyes lit up. This barbed wire was from a patent that Pete didn't have in his collection. He had amassed over 40 different types of patented, manufactured barbed wire of varying dates, and they were mounted on the wall in the entranceway. An intact 18-inch piece was all that was necessary to be museum quality, and Tracey's three-foot section of wire, when cut to that size, would fit perfectly into Pete's growing collection.

Pete exclaimed, "Treasured find, Tracey!"

Pete continued fingering through all the artifacts on the bar, fiddling with Wes's hand-forged nails, and scratching the side of the old brass shell casing he had found.

"Great discoveries, Wes!" praised Pete.

Julie had collected a chipped arrowhead and a small blue medicine bottle with the name "Dr. Wizard" molded into the glass on the side of the bottle. The bottle was a great find to display in a shadow box, and while the arrowhead wasn't museum condition, it would still be a great souvenir of Julie's Christmas visit. Pete lauded her efforts. Brad's prized .50 caliber lead musket ball turned out to be a pitted, worn-out iron ball bearing from an old wagon wheel hub, but no matter, it was Brad's effort that impressed Pete. Brad's effort didn't impress sister

Julie, however. She declared Brad's musket ball to be bogus and fraudulent, and said it should be judged as a very trivial and insignificant contribution from such an experienced outdoorsman, and that any true outdoorsmen would be ashamed of Brad's offering. The entire dump-digging crew, except Brad, roared in laughter and clapped in agreement.

Then Tracey pulled out of her pocket the small intact arrow point she had picked up off the slab in the riverbed and laid it on the bar, and the whole crew fell silent as Pete picked it up and rolled the arrowhead around in his fingers inspecting it. "It's perfect," Pete declared, and that verdict brought to an end the artifact judging. Tracey's discoveries of the pristine arrowhead and the collectable length of barbed wire quickly aroused Pete's attention, and for her keen eye and perseverance in the discovery of such treasures, Pete awarded Tracey the expedition's grand prize, which was nothing less than Granddaddy's public approval and announcement of her first-place finish. She was thrilled, and the crew heartily applauded Pete's final decision.

It wasn't the trinkets of unknown ancestries found underground that morning that made the day so special, but rather the discovery of priceless virtues that were nurtured and dug up from the roots of our own family tree: virtues of togetherness, love, joy, and happiness that were rediscovered that morning. This simple dig produced a sense of belonging, a feeling of fitting in, and it unearthed the wisdom and lore of the traditions that tied us all together. It loosed a kindred spirit lying dormant in the kids that would come forth and bind them as family as they explored the dumps and dug in the sand. It had been a great expedition of family fun and unity.

The cookhouse bell clanged, and it was time to eat. Everyone from the headquarters charged outside and plodded through the drifting snow and into the aromatic cookhouse. They lined up at the buffet and loaded their plates with piles of spaghetti, green salad, and hunks of garlic bread, then sat down to eat. It was a busy meal with the conversation buzzing back and forth, and the recollections of today's events retold. There was discussion of the upcoming talent show, and bets were being placed on who would flub their routine and who would shine forth as stars. The favorites to sparkle appeared to be the girls—Christine, Julie, and Tracey—who would perform as a trio and had rehearsed there routine in good faith. The boys—Wes, Brad, and little Pete—on the other hand, had goofed off and practiced very little, hoping to win by making fools of themselves, or hoping that the judges, Sally and Pete, would take pity and vote for them because they were so cute. The singers in both acts were slurping their spaghetti and actively promoting themselves, trying to persuade and smooth-talk Pete and Sally into voting for them. No dice. The judges wouldn't be swayed by charming blather; bribing wouldn't be a part of the decision making. When all were sated on spaghetti, there was still peach cobbler and homemade ice cream for dessert that would end a perfect meal. The family was stuffed, and they oozed out of the cookhouse and down the sidewalk toward the headquarters, drawn by the waft and warmth of the mesquite fire blazing inside. The kids stopped and frolicked outside, playing around in the drifting snow, and laughing as they threw snowballs at one another. What a beautiful white Christmas Eve it was! A delicious dinner was finished, and more fun was on the way.

The Christmas talent show was about to begin. Family spectators arranged themselves around the make-shift stage set up the entryway. Some of the family chose to watch the production from inside a bubbly hot tub, with a view out the atrium window of the soft falling snow. Others relaxed in chairs and sofas with their coffee and cordials to enjoy the performance, warming by the fire.

First out to perform were the girls: vivacious, beautiful, young women. The saucy trio slinked out on stage dancing and pantomiming to a recording of The Pointers Sisters' 1970s hit "Fire." The girls were dressed in flashy evening dresses, costume jewelry, and spiked heels, and their stage makeup looked flawless as they lip-synced to the music. The choreography was crisp and smooth and perfectly in step. Their practice had paid off; it was a flirtatious, snazzy act. Christine, the youngest, was the only vocalist who was actually singing along with the music, and, of course, she could be heard loudly and plainly. It was always difficult to keep Christine quiet, but no one wanted to quiet her at this moment. With her verve and character she nailed her role in the act, and was very entertaining. Go Christine! The girls were great dancers and their performance had the family clapping their hands and tapping their feet as they watched the three talented ladies strut their stuff. It was a class act, and they received a standing round of applause from all the family, especially the judges. Sally and Pete were thrilled with the girls' part in the talent show. What Christmas cheer! What spirit!

The boys had their work cut out for them. To win the competition they had to deliver the greatest performance of their lives. They chose a song with Christmas origins, "We Three Kings of Orient Are," an old noel written by a clergyman in 1857. It was a story about the Magi, the wise men, who journeyed from the East to announce the Christ child at his birth. As the boys came onstage they were wrapped in sheets and beach towels for their costumes, and shod in flip-flops, bare feet, and cowboy boots in place of sandals. They had picked strands of ivy from the yard, woven them into crowns, and wore the crowns scrunched down on their heads. Wes was armed with a stock whip stuck in his belt in place of a sword, and Brad carried a baseball bat for his staff. Pete's dog, a blue healer named Buck, was commandeered to act as the pack animal for the fumbling kings, and the dog had a big red bow tied around his neck. Little Pete was bribing Buck to stay close to the act by feeding him treats from his pocket. The boys had already forgotten most of words to the song as they began to sing, and all three were peering around one another trying to read from a single sheet of hand-scribbled notes. They were in sheer agony groping for the words to the song, and their singing was off key, but no matter. Wes was missing chords on the guitar too, but so what? Words or no words, on key or off key, chords or no chords, they just wanted to press on and get the act over with. These three kings were unpracticed imposters and they knew it. They had forgotten the words to the song, lost the melody, and their act had broken down. They had suffered long enough, and finally with great relief they finished their sorry song. The boys looked up slowly and sheepishly into the audience expecting boos and hisses from the crowd, but no, the family exploded in cheers and clapping, with all thumbs up, applauding and hollering for more Kings! Unexpectedly, the boys' agonizing struggle on stage was a riot, a huge success! Then the acts were judged. Pete voted for the girls as best act, and Sally voted for the boys simply because they were "just too cute to pass up." There wouldn't be a loser in the contest; first place was awarded to both acts and the competition was judged a tie, much to the chagrin of the girls. But the judges' decision was final, and the girls would just have to suck it up and wait for another Christmas. Christine and Buck's roles in the show were deemed the most outstanding, and they received special recognition from the judges for their stellar performances.

It had been a bustling day full of activities, and the ranch crew was tired. Some would stay up to relax in the hot tub; others would sit and chat while finishing their drinks. The majority headed to bed to rest in expectation of tomorrow. The snowstorm was over, and a beautiful white Christmas day would await the early morning risers.

The diehard coffee drinkers woke early and headed to the coffee pot. The ranch crew was already busy in the kitchen, starting breakfast and preparing the turkey and dressing for roasting. They were prepping fresh fruits and vegetables for assorted dishes, and there was a bustling of activity. It was a beautiful, pristine Christmas day, and a few early risers, grasping their coffee mugs, were gazing out the bar window, marveling at the six inches of fallen snow. The landscape had turned dazzling white, glistening in the early morning rays of sun that peeked through the Organ Mountains. The snow had changed the face of the land, covered ravines and washes and produced shadows that tricked the eye. It made the familiar hills look foreign. The early birds were sipping their coffee, eating Christmas cookies, and snapping pictures of this snowy expanse that was blanketing the terrain in all directions. The smell of bacon frying wafted from the cookhouse and signaled that breakfast was near. Slowly the family gathered in the cookhouse at the buffet line for portions of bacon, eggs, freshly patted tortillas, and jalapeno salsa to top it all off. They would eat heartily, then assemble in the headquarters around the Christmas tree to exchange the hand-made gifts.

Hand-made gifts were a family Christmas tradition. Each gift would have to be constructed from scratch and given to someone in the family whose name they had drawn a year earlier. Gifts were exchanged, and the creativity of the givers would be tested to see who could improvise the best, sometimes funniest present. First to open his gift was Brad; it was from Wes. Brad received a shoe scraper made from upside down bottle caps nailed onto a board. It would be ideal to scrape the mud off his boots after a long deer hunt! Little Pete had carved a slingshot out of a fork in a mesquite tree, fitted it with thick rubber slings, and he gave it to Christine, who was very vocal in her approval. Sister Joy gave me an old yellowing denture I had worn for many years and had given to her as a gift one Christmas. The denture replaced two of my bottom teeth that Joy had knocked out during a fight when we were kids. When I was refitted with a permanent bridge years ago, I gave her the two yellow teeth for her hand-made Christmas gift. I mounted the teeth in a shadow box, and she was delighted to receive them and to hang them on her wall at home in memory of her victory over me. This Christmas she gave me back the denture, which she had refashioned into a fancy tie tack, a tie tack that I would treasure forever and wear for special family occasions. It was a great conversation piece. Perhaps the best gift of the morning was what Brad gave to little Pete: a Frisbee—well, not actually a Frisbee, but a flat and perfectly round "meadow muffin" that had dried out in the pasture. It was the size of a dinner plate, an ideal size for playing catch. Brad scraped up the crappy little "muffin" from the pasture, spray-painted it gold, and gave it to little Pete. Pete loved his quirky new Frisbee and couldn't wait to get outside to toss it around. Such were the goofy gifts that the family would make and share with one another, crazy hand-made gifts that created rapturous hilarity and joy in the Christmas gathering. Gift opening was over, and it was time to move the party outside and enjoy the snow before it melted.

Soon everyone was outside frolicking in the snow or busy with chores. Pete was at the barn readying the horses for a ride in the snow, and the kids were playing football in the snowy headquarters pasture. Other folks were bundled up outside sipping coffee or hot toddies and enjoying the chilly but windless morning, watching the football players scramble in the snow. Little Pete was alone tossing his new Frisbee around—he couldn't find anyone who wanted to play catch with it! However, Pete would quickly forget the Frisbee, and the football players would quit their game, because it was time to saddle up for a horseback ride in the snow.

The grandkids hurried to the barn and currycombed and saddled their horses, anticipating a new experience horseback. Some had never ridden in the snow, and before they rode out Pete cautioned them about always walking the horses and staying on the roads when in deep snow. They were to avoid riding in the ravines or on the hillsides, and they were to keep a watch out for snow-covered holes that could stumble a horse and throw a rider. The terrain appeared different after a snowstorm. The ravines were flattened out and the peaks appeared higher. The reflection of the sun off the snow could be blinding, and the snowdrifts would cast new shadows that could trick the eye and affect depth perception. Walking their horses was Pete's rule for the kids today. The six riders rode west in the middle pasture following a rutted pipeline road that led over a saddle in the Sleeping Lady Hills. The kids were amazed by the grotesque shapes and strange transformations formed by the snow in the valleys and on the hillsides. It was like riding in a totally alien environment, icy slick and visually challenging. The snow, however, was a blessing. It would melt into the ground rather than run off in a rampage like a flash flood, and it would loosen up and provide moisture to the rocky soil that would sprout edible weeds during the early spring. Even blizzards were acceptable to the ranchers in this dry climate with unpredictable rainfall. Moisture in any form was precious in the high desert, and the grandkids were enjoying a thrilling horseback ride in the snow that had created this new white wilderness that was spread out ahead of them.

In an hour the kids had reached the saddle of the gap in the Sleeping Lady Hills, and they rested their horses, scanning the terrain both east and west and choosing their route. Carolyn and little Pete were the scoutmasters on this ride. They had made the ride before, and though young, they were good horsemen; they had helped gather cattle and do other cowboy work during the summer months and holidays they spent at the ranch. They also knew the lay of the land. They considered leading the crew around Reichey Butte, a half-mile to the west, and then head back east towards the headquarters, but the day was warming and the sun was already melting the snow. This didn't bode well for a horseback ride around the butte. It would be muddy and slick at the base of the butte, with cracked granite and jagged shale rock sticking up from the hard slippery slopes of the butte. It would be a slow and unsafe ride for an inexperience crew. Little Pete and Carolyn would heed Dad's advice and stick to riding in the roads. Pete had mentored them well. They rode down off the saddle and headed southwest, following the water line road until they reached the dirt road heading back to the headquarters about three miles to the east. This road had a sandy base and it was a safe stretch of road to loosen the reins, give the horses their heads, and walk at a faster pace. The horses liked the loose reins, and would walk faster because they were heading back to the headquarters to a manger full of hay and a can of oats. The kids enjoyed the scenery, the reminiscing about past Christmases, and the bragging about their ranch exploits and all the adventures they all had experienced on the Corralitos. It was one o'clock in the afternoon. The kids were hungry, the horses were hungry, and they all were hoofing it back to the headquarters at a brisk walk in the crisp, clean air.

The riders arrived at the ranch, unsaddled their horses and headed to the headquarters to continue their eventful Christmas day. The turkey was in the oven and smelling wonderful. The family was spread out in small groups in the entrance foyer and back bar relating stories and pouring over photo albums filled with recollections of memorable times on the ranch. Lois was playing the piano, and people were singing along. A few were relaxing in the bubbling hot tub. We would talk to Lawrence and Bertha and Howard and Blanche on the West Coast, and relatives everywhere. There was only one telephone line at the headquarters and it was busy all day with Christmas calls. The afternoon activity was subdued. As we waiting for dinner, some were packing their luggage for an early morning departure out of El Paso Airport. Family would be leaving tomorrow, and plans had to be made for the next reunion. The hilarious gatherings in the previous days were replaced this afternoon with conversations, face-to-face get-togethers and sisterly discussions. This chitchat would summarize the latest Christmas events and happenings that would add to the family lore, and enrich the lode of priceless memories in our legacy. We continued talking together as we ate and enjoyed our Christmas dinner, and were thankful our family was still strong and intact.

The next day was spent hauling family to the airport to return to their homes, schools, and work, and the Corralitos crew would adjust back to a normal ranching routine. Christmas at the Corralitos had been fun and spiritually en-riching. The ranch was the hub of the family unit. It was the geographical center of the spread out families, and a nucleus of teaching and tradition that bound us together. There was no better training for kids than to spend summers at the ranch working and taking part in everyday activities. It was a simple, unadorned life-style, filled with never ending responsibilities that spawned character, creativity, and a work ethic in the kids. And there were no greater mentors of these priceless attributes than Pete and Sally. Their hands-on approach of teaching by example required cooperation among the children, and the kids respected and trusted Mom and Dad for demanding it. Christmas was over this year, but the raising of kids was never over. These Christmases were important in strengthening our family unity and enriching our lives.

7

Flood and Drought

Snow was beautiful that Christmas, and moisture was always welcome on the Corralitos, whether in the form of snow or rain showers. But if strong thunderstorms produced rain that fell so fast and furiously that it couldn't soak into the ground, they could produce torrents of runoff water in the form of dangerous, destructive flash floods that would sweep down from the mountains in the ravines and canyons. The floods would engulf the draws and lowlands with swift-moving rivers of muddy water and debris, and could paralyze and isolate any ranching operation until the floodwater subsided. Such was our predicament one morning during a roundup in late September of 1979 at the Candler Corrals in the Mason Draw, eight miles northwest of the headquarters.

It was cold and blustery, with the temperature near freezing that morning as eight cowboys unloaded their horses from trailers. We would be gathering the South Adobe and Mason pastures to the far west of the ranch along the boundary fence line, and pushing the cattle five miles east to the Candler Corrals for processing. We were seasoned cowboys, not a greenhorn in the bunch, and with our crew we could easily gather the 300 head of cattle in the pastures in two or three hours—that is, if the weather cooperated. A front approaching from the northwest was due to arrive soon, and we didn't know what to expect from the weather. We separated and rode north and south and spread out behind the cattle, then began gathering them in from the foothills and heading them east toward the corrals. There were ravines and small canyons at the base of the Uvas Mountains that the cowboys had to search out for cattle. The crew scoured the hillsides kicking out cattle, then began their drive east to the Candler Corrals, sweeping back and forth behind the scattered herd as they headed down Mason Draw towards the corrals. Cowboys were also pushing cattle from the south up the draw towards the corrals. Mason Draw was the center of the drainage area between the Uvas Mountains to the west and the Sleeping Lady Hills to the east, with Magdalena Peak forming a northern boundary of the horseshoe-shaped watershed. The runoff water from these mountains drained through Mason Draw, then out the mouth of the horseshoe and into the sand hills south of the interstate highway. The draw—eleven miles long and ten miles wide—drained water from over a hundred square miles of pasture. The area was geologically perfect for collecting a lot of runoff from the surrounding mountains, and Mason Draw was notorious for flash floods.

The weather was rapidly deteriorating, the storm growing in intensity. We had gathered cattle for an hour and were halfway to the corrals with most of the cattle out ahead of us when the sky opened up with torrents of rain from a thunderstorm of unexpected intensity. It began to rain heavily, and cold sixty-mile-an-hour wind gusts raked us from the north. There was lightning, and every direction was closing in with roiling, foreboding black clouds. It was a torrential thunderstorm. The rain limited vision to a hundred feet, and the cowboys and the horses had no cover. I was drenched: my boots, chaps, saddle and rigging, all were saturated. I had a poncho, but it offered little protection against the blasting rain and the strong, ripping winds.

The gullies and small ravines at the base of the mountains began filling up and streaming south, swelling in size and growing in intensity. This rush of water off the mountains spilled into the larger ravines, then flooded into Mason Draw, where it grew in size and force as it rampaged south. The flood came in waves and walls of muddy, turbulent water, some five feet high, rushing down the ravines and arroyos, carrying with it jumbled masses of stumps and brush. The torrent ripped off huge chunks of earth from the ravine embankments as it rumbled downhill with a force strong enough to knock a train off its tracks. The weather was too violent; it was a dangerous situation. The relentless wind and rain had buffeted and pelted the cowboys long enough, and they reluctantly let their scattering cattle go and rode to higher, safer ground to avoid the rising flood waters. The cattle I was pushing were scattering out ahead of me seeking higher ground, and were impossible to control. I quit the cattle and rode quickly to the top of the nearest knoll. It was difficult to see through the torrent of rain, and dangerous to leave the knoll and cross the raging water now encircling me. The water was too swift and unpredictable. I was stranded on high ground like the other riders, isolated on a high spot and relieved to be out of the flooding, but still caught in a drenching thunderstorm and bone-chilling wind. By seeking refuge high up on the knoll, I was a prime target for a lightning strike. I could hear the thunder clap, and I could see the lightning in the distance. But worrying about the lightning was useless. There was nothing I could do about it. I was stranded by the floodwater on a high patch of ground, and could only wait out the storm, let the water recede, and try to stay warm.

The storm began to subside after dropping three inches of rain in less than an hour, but the runoff in the ravines was still rising. The buffeting wind was bitterly cold, especially wearing soggy clothing, and as I tried to stay warm, thoughts raced through my mind: Were the other cowboys safe? Were the trucks and trailers moved out of the draw before the flood hit? And another big question: Did the new earthen dams built by Pete along the draw hold together and not wash away? I pondered these things as I sat in the saddle, wet from my hat down to my boots, shivering in the cold wind, and waiting for the water to subside.

As the clouds lifted I could make out the colored ponchos of the cowboys in the distance descending from their high spots, and navigating around the rain-swollen ravines, wending their way back to the corrals. Because of the ferocious storm, none were able to gather any cattle, and all of the riders were wet to the core and very cold. The cowboys needed to escape the cold wind, find a warm spot, and dry out. I couldn't cross the deep water in the ravines from where I was, so I left my high perch and headed south along the draw to find a wide spot where the water had flattened out and it was possible to wade my horse across to get to the corrals. I finally crossed the draw in a wide, sandy spot still flowing with three inches of water, and met up with Pete and Lawrence on the hillside. They were just as wet and miserable as I was, and we turned and rode north against a cold wind toward the corrals, thoroughly defeated in our cattle drive, but happy to be out of the deluge we had just experienced.

The ground crew had done their jobs, and the women from the headquarters were also on hand to meet the cold, wet cowboys with towels, hot drinks, and food when they made it back to the corrals. They brought warm, dry jackets for those that needed them. The women had heard we were in a flood, and they drove seven miles to the corrals prepared to help in any way when the riders made it back. The ranch crew had moved the pickups and trailers out of the flood plain earlier before the storm hit, and had parked them at the corrals in a circle to block the wind. Then they built a big bonfire in the center of the circle to warm up and dry out the cowboys and their gear. The heaters were warming the cabs in the idling pickups, and the ground crew was ready to receive the waylaid cowboys

We had been in the saddle exposed to the rain and cold for more than three hours before we finally rode into the Candler Corrals. We were stiff and numb from the cold. We stripped off our wet jackets and chaps and warmed ourselves by the bonfire. Some sat in the heated cabs of the pickups, sipping hot coffee and drying out. The bosses decided not to regather the pasture today. The heavy rain and flooding of Mason Draw had scattered the cattle, and we would let them settle down for a couple of days; then when the water had subsided we would come back in and round up the pasture. Thanks to the alert ground crew, the cowboys were able to dry out, warm up, and eat some hot food. The cowboy crew was eager to get back to work, and there was processing to do at the headquarters, but before they left the Candler corrals, they spread flakes of hay out in the corrals and opened the gates to attract cattle that they would gather again in two days. There was rarely any slack time when working a roundup, and the cowboys liked it that way.

The morning that had started out so badly turned out wonderfully. Pete in a four-wheel-drive pickup navigated the muddy roads back into the new dam sites and reported back to the crew that the all the new dams had withstood the flood and were full of water, the largest of them backing up water for more than half a mile. All the dams were intact with water flowing over the spillways; that was a beautiful sight for Pete to see, and was a great resource for the ranch. The dams would hold enough livestock water to last a year without replenishment. The flood had soaked the thirsty earth and would produce copious amounts of forage this spring and summer on 75,000 acres of prime pasture that cattle and wildlife would thrive on. The rain event that had started out as a curse on the cowboys ended up being a blessing to the ranch. Pete was overjoyed with the outcome.

In accomplishing his projects, like the construction of the 52 earthen dams, Pete established a close working relationship with the governing authorities of the grazing lands and the water resources: The Bureau of Land Management, which issued permits to graze cattle on the public lands; the State Land Office, from whom we leased over 50,000 acres of grazing land; and the State Engineers Office, which administered the water laws, issued permits to drill new wells, and was responsible for the adjudication of water rights. Before Pete began any of his major projects, the regulatory agencies would be notified, and they would give us their written approval. The policies of the agencies were administered through field offices in Las Cruces and at New Mexico State University. The people who worked with us were dedicated public servants who became friends over the years. They were hands-on workers ready to assist the ranch in improving the resources. The cooperation of all the land- and water-governing agencies was outstanding. Our combined efforts added value to all the lands, public and private, and the ranch's success was their success. It was a win-win relationship. Our contacts in the agencies were people who knew the land, and knew its history. Most of them were long-time residents of the area, and they respected our efforts to improve the dry desert with the development of water resources. During their visits to the ranch, Pete and Sally would often invite them to the headquarters for lunch and discuss the ranching activities and any new regulatory developments. The field workers were knowledgeable and would spend long, tireless hours helping us with our projects. We, in turn, would visit their homes in the valley for barbecues and activities that would include their friends and associates. These agencies— and especially the people who administered them—were a valuable resource. We appreciated their efforts, applauded their work, and enjoyed their company. Their cooperation was crucial to our success in ranch development.

The headquarters was always a center of activity. Lawrence and Howard would visit the ranch often. When Bertha and Blanche were with them, Barbara and Sally would take the ladies to Old Mesilla shopping for the latest deals in western wear. The bosses would drive out on the ranch, inspecting the various projects Pete had underway and thoroughly enjoying each other's company.

All the men loved progress, and there had been progress under Pete's management. Lawrence and Bertha had racehorses stabled at Ruidoso Downs Racetrack, and would stay at the ranch and then spend the weekends during the racing season in their motor home parked in the high pines at the quarterhorse races. They loved the races, and when possible we would drive up to meet them and watch the ponies run and enjoy the day. These were times of great activity and accomplishment at the ranch, days of happiness. The bosses, even in their advancing years, were as active as young pups, and rode their horses often. They loved their horses. Lawrence and Howard kept horses at the ranch to ride when they came. Pete had two horses that he rode, and he kept a stud horse in the barn that he hired out for breeding purposes. Horses were a part of their lives.

As Lawrence aged he quieted—he was not as unchecked and unbridled. He was more predictable in his actions and much easier to abide. He had settled down. Pete's influence and the passage of time were mellowing Lawrence. I felt closer to him, but I was still wary, waiting for the next time he might unleash another verbal barrage on some unsuspecting person. He was a very influential, generous man, but his mouth had gotten him in trouble with decent people, and he had lost friends because of it. Lawrence was able to ruin a lifetime of friendship with one caustic outburst; he would never apologize, but he ended up remorseful, and agonized over his own conduct. Now there seemed to be a lessening of his rude behavior, and I felt more comfortable being around him than at any other time in my life.

Sally and Barbara were always busy with work and projects. Mom's real-estate business was prospering, and she had two agents working for her in her Las Cruces office selling properties. She was on a constant go with her business as well as tending to ranch duties: buying groceries for the ranch crew, running ranch errands, and hauling parts and equipment in and out of El Paso and Las Cruces. Mother believed in the old adage, "Idle hands are the devil's workshop," and she was continually scurrying here and there between her real-estate business and the ranch business. Barbara, too, shared much of the ranch responsibilities with Sally. She was diligent with every project, never idle, and if not busy with necessary ranch work, she always had projects under way. She loved making beautiful stained-glass lamps, and with her knack for decoration, she renovated the interior of the headquarters. Her work in the restoration and beautification of the headquarters was her continual gift to the ranch. Barbara was a great organizer of people and events. Before coming to the ranch, she had worked for years with the State Fair of Texas, the largest fair in the United States. She was their organizer, their go-to person, handling parades and special events. She understood the crowd-control issues, the route planning, and the hands-on coordination necessary to make parades and festival events successful. Just as important, she knew the people and the resources to contact to make it happen. This valuable experience would be helpful in 1981 when she volunteered her time and effort assisting the City of Las Cruces in sponsoring its first large city event.

In collaboration with the city, she would lead in creating an event that would include the largest gathering of people in the history of the Las Cruces, the first annual Whole Enchilada Fiesta. When it came to creating a festive happening, Barbara knew the entertainment business and loved being involved. She was an innovative, determined, and spirited young woman.

***

Of the three weather disasters that impact cattle ranching in the southwest—floods, blizzards, and drought—drought is by far the worst. It can decimate cowherds, force the liquidation of ranch holdings, create bankruptcies, and tear apart families struggling to survive its parching grip. Drought was the bane of every rancher, especially in the vast southwestern desert. It was the worst calamity that could befall a cattle ranch.

In 1978 and 1979 the Corralitos suffered severe drought conditions. Only trace amounts of rainfall fell during this time, and it was dry as a bone in the high desert for two lingering years. In the first stages of drought, grasses lacking moisture can't grow and reseed, and in a year's time the native vegetation would be cropped close to the ground by the restless, hungry cattle. Seeds didn't sprout, nothing green could be seen poking through the scorched earth, and without rain there would be no nutritious weeds to forage during the spring. Only the mesquite could flourish. Sometimes during droughts the mesquite produced a large bean crop that the cattle would readily eat, but the beans wouldn't last forever, and they would add only a small amount of the total nutrition the starving cattle would need. The 52 earthen dams would eventually go dry, slowly receding and leaving thick, sticky mud that spread out and opened up with deep cracks when it dried. The mud was a death trap to cattle.

When strong winds blew, they raked the dry, parched earth and formed choking red clouds of dust that covered the landscape and dwellings and obscured vision. Swarms of biting black flies spawned by the dry, dusty conditions pestered the cattle relentlessly. With less forage, cows began losing weight and gave birth to smaller, weaker calves, and some cows—because of their poor nutrition—failed to have a calf. Cattle were forced to range further in search of forage, which caused additional stress and weight loss. Older cattle were the most vulnerable, especially old cows nursing calves, because a cow's energy requirement was greater for milk production; with the loss of forage, the older cows with calves were the first to suffer. Bulls lost weight, too. They became weak and gaunt searching for feed, and they lost their virility. Some would isolate themselves in canyons, not seeking out cows to breed, and this would cut short next year's calf crop. There was sufficient drinking water for the cattle. Pete's expansion of the water lines, the building of new dams, and the addition of new drinkers provided sufficient water for the cattle even in the most remote areas, but after a year of drought the problem was a lack of forage, not drinking water. The result was that the cattle were constantly in search of something to eat, losing weight and vitality every day. Drought was a devastating plague.

The drought greatly increased the workload at the ranch as we kept a vigil on our suffering livestock. The cowboys were in the saddle many hours, and the ground crew was hauling hay daily out to the cattle in the pastures. Water lines and drinkers were reinspected, and anything leaking precious water was fixed. Every dam and dirt tank on the ranch would be checked daily for cattle that might be mired in the mud. The alfalfa haying operation was the ranch's greatest asset during the drought. We loaded pickups and a flat rack truck with ten tons of baled hay, and hauled it daily to the outer pastures where we would spread it out at different water locations to supplement the dwindling forage. We spread hay in every corral to lure the cattle inside where we could feed the animals, inspect them, and haul them to the headquarters if necessary. If we could gather the weak cattle into the corrals, we could feed them hay and save them from starvation. In the corrals we could also load the weakest cows and their baby calves and haul them to the headquarters, where they would be penned and fed continually. The cowboys rode through the pastures, searching out the ravines and isolated spots for cattle that they would gather, and then slowly pushed the cattle toward the haying locations. As the cowboys gathered the drought-stricken herd, a few of the older, weaker cows would tire out, stop in their tracks and lie down, refusing to go any further. For such downed cattle, we hauled hay in four-wheel-drive pickups. We spread hay out beside them, hoping that after a rest they would be able to stand up, eat enough hay to gain strength, and then continue on alone to the feeding locations. If the cows didn't rise to their feet soon, their legs would go numb and become paralyzed, and they would never walk again. When this happened, and we were certain the cows couldn't rise and walk, we did the humane thing and shot the animals. We dragged their carcasses with a chain behind a pickup to the nearest ravine and left them there to be consumed by the coyotes and buzzards. Within two weeks there was nothing left of the carcasses but scattered bones and patches of hide and hair. What a loss! Every cow represented hundreds of dollars of investment, not counting the time and effort required to maintain her, and to lose valuable animals in such a cruel and meaningless way was gut-wrenching and heartbreaking. Any surviving orphaned calves of the dead cows would be roped, put in trailers, and brought to the headquarters to be fed, and the smaller calves would be hand-fed with bottles of formula twice daily until they could be weaned and were able to eat hay.

The dirt dams were a boon to the cattle when they were full of water, but when in the grips of a drought and drying up, they were a death-trap to a few poor, unlucky, old cows. When healthy, the old cows could normally wade in and out of the water easily, and slog through the narrow mudflats at the perimeter of the tanks without a problem. The flats were wider now during the drought, and the cows were weak from hunger. During the night, when the cows tried to cross the mud flats to get to the receding pool of water in the center of the tank, they got stuck in the flats. After a few minutes of struggling with all four feet mired in the mud, they would sink deeper into the mud, sometimes up to their bellies. When we found them in the morning it was normally too late to save them.

Using chains and ropes to reach the bogged-down cows, we would pull them out of the mud, but usually it was too late. They were weak and couldn't stand; their legs had become paralyzed overnight, and they wouldn't survive. The downed cows would be shot and dragged into the ravines. Any calves would be roped and brought to the headquarters. It was pitiful and thankless work having to destroy your own livestock, but the drought knew no favorites, livestock or man. For the cowboys, having to kill the cattle that they tended and cared for over many months was not an easy task. It was a bitter pill to swallow.

Our nurse cow was a blessing. She was an old cow in good condition that we had gathered from the pasture after her calf had died. Her bag was full of milk, and the old cow would accept other calves to nurse, which was unusual. She was a marvel at the amount of milk she could produce when fed high-quality hay and rolled oats. She was able to nurse nine baby calves and keep them alive. The baby calves, especially the newborn, needed to receive colostrum, the protein-rich kind of milk that a cow produces after she gives birth; it's also rich in antibodies, so it gives a newborn calf immunity against disease. Without colostrum, newborn calves would die, usually within a few days. The orphaned calves the cowboys collected from the pastures were gathered at the headquarters and systematically put in with the old cow for fifteen minutes a day to nurse. The crew rotated nine calves to nurse on the old lactating cow, who was penned tightly in a stall so she couldn't move and kick, and the calves could nurse more easily. The old cow didn't mind two or three of the suckling calves nursing at one time. She was busy eating her fill of nutritious fodder and producing gallons of milk a day. After nursing on the cow for a couple of days, the calves would be bottle-fed by hand twice daily. When they were old enough to wean from the bottle, the calves were switched to a hay diet and eventually put back out to pasture. The old cow and her wonderful colostrums saved nine baby calves that would have died during the drought without her precious milk full of life-saving antibodies.

There was no way to anticipate a drought, nor its duration, and there was no sure-fire plan to fully protect your livestock when one occurred. Every grazing scheme on the ranch depended on rainfall, and no rain for two years spelled disaster. A mere inch of rainfall during the drought would have changed everything. An inch of rain would have sprouted seeds and native grasses. Succulent weeds would have shot up overnight and covered the rusty landscape with a blanket of verdant, lime-green growth. Within a few days, there would be plenty of green feed, and the forage conditions would rapidly improve and put an end to the starvation. But such a rain did not occur, and the drought persisted.

Ranching was a roll of the dice. The rancher invested his money and resources and was betting that a drought wouldn't occur, but in nature's weather cycles it always did. The rancher understood the possibility of drought and assumed the risk. He knew that if he ranched long enough, he would suffer a drought, and he would probably not be ready for it. But when a drought did occur, what did the rancher do? Did he gather the herd and sell them? Or did he keep his cattle and hang on? Relocating the herd would be expensive, and it would be stressful on the cattle. And with other ranchers selling their drought-stricken cattle, there would be an over-supply, less demand, and the price would be low when you sold. It would also be a slow, tedious process to gather the starving herd, and some of the older cattle would not survive. And after the drought was over, the rancher would have to replace his breeding animals at a time when every other rancher affected by the drought was replacing his herd, so because of demand the market price of replacements would be sky-high. This law of supply and demand would force many ranchers out of business during the drought. We held on and tended to our ravaged herd at the headquarters' corrals and out in the pastures. We were fortunate at the ranch that we had the haying operation to supplement our range cattle. On the flip side of the coin, we lost much revenue feeding the hay to our own cattle and not selling hay to the dairies as a cash crop. But it was a better outcome for us to feed our cattle, because we didn't have to gather and sell any starving cattle at a low price. After a year of drought, the Corralitos was holding its own, coping with the sere conditions one day at a time. We continued the miserable, dusty work of hauling hay to our cattle daily, and we tried to save all the compromised animals we could, gathering them into the headquarters or feeding them in the pastures. This drought would be expensive no matter what course of action the ranch pursued, and any plan to combat the drought had indefinite costs and inherent risks.

There were never any easy answers or sure paths to follow during a drought. The ranchers tried to minimize their losses and do the best they could with the resources they had to work with. The constant refrain from the cowboys during this horrible dry spell was, "We need some rain!" At the hardware store the conversation of the ranchers and the locals who shopped there was focused on rain, or the lack of it. Everyone was affected economically: the ranchers, the farmers, and the businessmen, and their lament was the same: "We just need a good rain!" In times of drought the ranchers dreamed of rain, and every fiber of their being was hoping and praying for rain. But this waiting and worrying over the possibility of a rainstorm would only lead to further indecision, and soon the ranchers were caught in a quandary of doubt about what to do in a situation that had no sure choices or solutions. Most of the ranchers held on. Everyone just held on one more day, toiling with the cattle and waiting for rain, praying for one good rain. That is all it would take. And the drought lingered on.

The first rainstorm began with an inch and a half of monsoon rain that fell all over the ranch and drenched the parched pastures during the first week of July. Within days there were two more storms packed with life-saving rain that showered down on the flats and draws and restored the sear, withered land. The ravines and gullies flowed red with runoff water, streamed into the dams, and filled them to capacity. Green weeds sprouted all over the ranch, and the native grasses, cropped short by the cattle during the drought, came to life and began to grow. The hungry cattle readily grazed on the greening pastures and regained their strength. There was finally a rest and relief from the two years of agonizing work on the Corralitos.

It had been a daunting experience contending with the drought. The drought was an invisible adversary that was impossible to defeat, like an illness that must run its course, and we suffered in its merciless grip for two distressful years. We were fortunate. We had the resources and an experienced crew to withstand the physical and financial upheaval caused by the drought. Pete's ground crew and the cowboys did an exemplary job in helping the ranch avert financial disaster: scouring the pastures for weak animals, hauling hay to the remote areas, bottle-feeding calves, struggling with weak cattle, and slogging out on foot into waist-deep muck to pull out cows that were mired in the mud flats. It was an immense effort for a handful of dedicated workers. The ranch only lost thirty head of cattle to the drought, and all of them were old weak cows that died while we were trying to save them. Our neighbors' losses were greater, and some of them were forced out of business. We were fortunate that we had Howard's and Lawrence's sound financial backing.

And the ladies at the headquarters worked tirelessly. Their contribution to the drought relief was immediate and immense; they did the thankless, necessary work that kept the ranch functioning during this turbulent time. They were tireless gofers, hauling supplies and groceries and feeding an overworked, worn out crew. The women were an integral part of the ranching operation, and the successful recovery from the drought was due in a great part to their hands-on involvement. The land would replenish and the ranch would be back to full capacity as soon as the grazing conditions permitted, and for that we were thankful. The drought had been an anguishing period of ranching history.

8

Pete

The drought was not the greatest calamity to befall the ranch during my life there. It was Pete's death that shocked and stunned the family. Dad died suddenly of a massive heart attack on the afternoon of Saturday, December 11, 1982. He had just got in from work and was sitting on the bed talking with Mother, and suddenly he made one small gasp, lay over on the bed, and lapsed unconscious. Mother frantically called us on the telephone, and we rushed across the pasture to the headquarters to his bedroom. We tried to revive him with heart pumping and breathing mouth to mouth, but he never gasped again or took another breath, and he never regained consciousness. We worked frantically with him trying to revive him until the ambulance arrived from Las Cruces and transported him to the hospital. The doctors in the emergency room did all they could do to save his life, but to no avail. Pete had passed away.

The anguish immediately following Pete's death was crushing and disorienting. Mother, Barbara and I were all overwhelmed with gripping, inescapable sorrow and wave upon wave of suffocating, relentless grief. I was numb and bewildered, trying to comfort Mother and needing comforting myself. I felt drained and empty, as if the most precious thing in life had been snatched from me, and I felt nothing but despair and sadness. I had suffered the death of my closest friend in a car accident years earlier, but that sadness was nothing compared to the agony of Pete's sudden death. Mother was confused with grief and denial, and exhausted from the ordeal. Barbara and I gathered close with her trying to sooth her sobbing and wailing, but relief from the despair was only momentary, and again she would begin her mournful weeping. Happiness and gaiety had fled the headquarters. There was no bustling or activity, only the huddling and consolation of three agonizing souls trying to internalize the immense loss they had just suffered. At moments I wanted to soothe and comfort Mother and Barbara, then at moments I just wanted to flee to a dark place and sit in a corner undisturbed, suffering alone with my grief. But sitting and doing nothing was not possible. Until Lawrence and Howard arrived, I needed to oversee the vital ranch activities: the livestock must be tended to and the fields must be irrigated. The ranch crew, though deeply saddened at Pete's death, would pitch in and steadfastly continue the necessary work during this difficult time of family mourning.

The notification of the family was the most difficult thing I had ever done in my life. The telephone calls to my sisters were filled with wild shrieks of horror, gasps of disbelief, and anguished cries of despair. And telling Howard, Lawrence and other close friends of the sad news of Pete's death was equally difficult. When all the family heard of Pete's passing, they rushed to the ranch to comfort one another and mourn his loss. Pete and Sally's dearest friends from the Mesilla valley, Hank and Chris Webb, arrived at the ranch within three hours of Pete's death, and took over the headquarters responsibilities of cooking, running errands, and answering the constant barrage of telephone calls. This act of kindness by Pete and Sally's closest friends would help ease the stress on the family, and give the family time to gather and mourn the loss of their beloved Pete without interruption.

Within thirty-six hours, Lawrence and Bertha, Howard and Blanche, and all the immediate family had arrived at the ranch, all of them entering the headquarters with grief and gloominess etched in their sad faces. Howard and Lawrence were both bereaved. The two were withdrawn and melancholy, and the distress of Pete's death showed in their haggard, tired faces. They had lost their best friend, a cousin, no different than a beloved brother, and they were distraught. Lawrence was meek as a lamb, and suffering the loss of his best earthly friend, his advisor, and his loyal helper in all things. He was subdued and humbled by Pete's death. Howard, too, was devastated. I saw him outside the headquarters, alone, leaning against the fence post with tears in his eyes, and he was as forlorn as I had ever seen him. He was, perhaps, just sharing one last moment, one last conversation with his beloved Pete.

There was sadness everywhere. The grandchildren felt deprived of their precious grandfather and were grieving too. They didn't want to ride their cherished horses until after Pete's funeral. They felt too depressed to saddle up until Pete was laid to rest. It was as if all activity had ceased and everyone's attention was focused on the memory of Pete. Each was reflecting on his own personal experiences and recollections of his hero, Pete. Some were holding in their grief, some were expressing it, but all of them were feeling it. There wasn't a dry eye on the ranch.

Pete's funeral was held in Las Cruces, and was well attended by family and close friends who came to say their final farewell to him. He was entombed at a hillside cemetery overlooking the bountiful Mesilla Valley at the foot of the west mesa. It was a beautiful and peaceful place to be laid to rest. After a few days there was an acceptance of Pete's death by his loved ones, and though still saddened, they would unite as family and continue ahead in their everyday lives and build upon Pete's incomparable legacy of love, loyalty and accomplishment.

After the funeral Lawrence and Howard asked me if I wanted to manage the ranch, and though hesitant about my decision, I agreed to take over as manager. My greatest uncertainty in taking the job was if I could get along with Lawrence without Pete's beneficial influence. For me to be able to manage the ranch, it was imperative that Lawrence, Howard and I communicate on an ongoing basis, and I would need to keep them up to date on current ranch activities. They would make the major decisions, and I would oversee the daily ranch work. Barbara would be hired to keep the books, do the payroll and to assist in necessary ranch activities. It was a daunting task for Barbara and me to take over Dad and Mom's responsibilities, but we were a good team and we would do our best. I would continue on as manager of the Corralitos for seven years with Pete's perseverance, accomplishments, and loyalty to his employers, as my benchmarks.

Sally would soon leave the ranch. She still grieved for Pete, but there were too many memories of Pete and their togetherness at the Corralitos for her to be happy any longer with the isolation of the ranching life. Mom chose wisely not to suffer that dark solitude and loneliness, and rather share herself with her family. She would turn over a new chapter in her life. She sold her real estate business in Las Cruces and moved to Las Vegas, Nevada. There she would be closer to more of her entire family, especially the grandchildren on the west coast. She, like Pete, was a mentor of children and would spend her golden years involved in the grandkids' activities, nurturing them, and giving unselfishly of herself to her flourishing family. Mom would often return to the ranch to enjoy the Christmas celebrations and other family gatherings. Her love, hard work and determination had bulwarked Pete's outstanding achievements throughout his life, and in her own endeavors she had many personal and business successes that would inspire any young woman to pursue excellence. Mom was a devoted wife and mother, and she and Pete's marriage was the ideal for many young families. She had a hands-on, practical approach to living, loving, and working. Her love and her tireless, energetic spirit would certainly be missed and never forgotten at the Corralitos.

A few days after Pete's interment, after we all had time to gather our thoughts, the family took a horseback ride in Pete's honor. Nine riders saddled and hauled their horses to a remote canyon in the Sleeping Lady Hills, six miles from the headquarters, and there we began a ride back to the headquarters in tribute to our beloved Pete. It was a cold December morning, and soft flakes of snow were floating down in the crisp, still, air as we mounted our horses and slowly rode out of the canyon and down toward the distant corrals. We talked and reminisced about our individual, unique experiences we had shared with Dad, the treasured times when he took each of us as his special person to instruct and enjoy our company. He loved to hear about our aspirations, our ambitions and dreams; he was a master at helping us deal with our problems. All of us at one time had received Pete's gift of love and mentoring, and the riders would share these precious recollections with each other. These candid, sometimes tearful conversations among the riders told of the profound influence Pete had in our lives. As we rode slowly towards the corrals, our talk changed from sad, whispered discussions, to refreshing accounts and light-hearted bantering, each of us telling the happy memories shared with Pete.

The sorrowful, ruddy faces of the cowboys soon broke into broad, happy smiles, and the sounds of chuckling and revelry arose from the riders as they headed down into the valley. There was a lifting of spirit in Pete's cowboy crew, and as we continued on they began joking and laughing with one another, re-counting Pete's incredible antics. The sadness had vanished in the riders; now there were only happy thoughts and jocular outbursts of relief and happiness. It was a jubilation of Pete's life and a celebration of his victory. It was as if Pete himself was riding in the midst of the crew, and prodding us to quit the sobbing and sorrow and be happy, to rejoice with him. He was in a far better place, and this was his parting message to us: Love one another. Be strong in mind and body, and arise in the morning and fit yourself to face another day. Pete had fought the good fight, and had excelled in life's most important matters. His legacy of goodness and manliness was now complete and entrusted to his progeny. When we finally arrived at the barn, we were all rejuvenated in spirit, and the suffering was gone. With Dad's tribute starting in such sadness and escalating into unbridled happiness, it was the greatest and most inspiring horseback ride I had ever taken.

9

Manager

I would miss Dad's presence, but the years of teaching and hands-on instruction he had given me would remain with me forever. His work ethic and zeal to get things done was exemplary, and I would use what he had taught me to accomplish the necessary work as ranch manager. Pete's mentoring would be the roadmap and compass to guide me in the right direction, and help me make the best decisions along the way.

Pete had constructed the dams and sunk the wells necessary to capture huge amounts of precious water, but the work he started wasn't yet complete. The state of New Mexico was negotiating with the landowners, the federal government, and the other states over ownership of the water above and below the ground in New Mexico. The state of New Mexico was trying to retain as much of the water as possible for its citizens, and there was impetus for landowners to list all the sources of water, both above and below ground, that they were putting to beneficial use, and document these sources with the State Engineer's Office. In the future, there would be a declaration of the water right, or water owned by the landowners, of a specified number of acre-feet of water that the landowner could use beneficially, and this ownership would depend on the landowners' past and current water usage. This declaration of beneficial use would include the 52 new earthen dams Pete had constructed, and the irrigation wells at the headquarters. It was necessary on the Corralitos to locate and document the sources of water everywhere we impounded it or pumped it for irrigation or livestock use.

My first undertaking as manager was to locate these water sources and document their size and quantity. With me was Tom, the field agent for the State Engineers Office, and my loyal friend Jake, a crusty, keen-eyed survivor of the World-War-II trenches, and a staunch supporter of the ranching projects, especially the development of water sources. Jake had an economic interest in the ranch. He stocked small minnows in our dams, and when they grew and matured he seined them from the dams and sold the minnows as live baitfish in Las Cruces. He was an excellent outdoorsman who understood the lay of the land and how to use a topographic map and compass. He knew the ranch and had driven or walked over every part of it; his keen eyes would be extremely useful in documenting the water sources.

The three of us began our water documentation at the headquarters wells. Tom was the official scribe. With an electronic probe he measured the depths of the wells, note the horsepower rating of the electric motors, and paced off the radii of the alfalfa circles to determine their size. He recorded his findings in an official logbook. These measurements would determine our beneficial use of the groundwater, and in the future when the basin was declared, we would own and be allowed to pump this quantity of underground water. The documentation at the headquarters required only a couple of days to complete, and during this time Barbara prepared hot meals at the headquarters for the hungry survey crew to devour and enjoy. For the next two weeks we ate sack lunches in a pickup somewhere out on the ranch as we searched for the brass caps and noted the legal descriptions of the dams.

Brass caps were actually brass rods that were driven deep into the ground at the corners of each section of land. The brass rods had flattened heads with their geographic locations stamped on the head. Finding these outlying brass caps was difficult. The caps had been driven in place 45 years earlier, each of them one mile from the neighboring cap, and some were no longer visible, having been covered with sand or by mesquite thickets or completely washed away by flash floods. Finding the caps was a challenge, requiring hands-on orientation skills with the maps, keen eyesight, knowledge of the terrain, and persistence in the search. A few brass caps had been found earlier, most by cowboys out tending cattle on the range, and when they found a brass cap the cowboys would mark it with piles of rocks, mesquite limbs, or whatever material was at hand. There were no global positioning satellites at that time; all of the measurements were taken from the ground to establish the location of the dams. Topographic maps containing the ranges, townships, and sections were used to determine the approximate location of the brass caps, with the maps showing surface features of the terrain such as hills, mountains, elevations and drainage patterns. Using the maps, we could approximate the location of the caps, and then we searched each area in pickups and on foot to locate them.

The search for the brass caps required two arduous weeks of riding in four-wheeled vehicles and also scouring the land on foot. If the caps weren't visible from the pickup, we had to get out and walk with shovels, poking and digging around in the rocky earth for usually a half hour until one of us found the buried cap by hitting it with a shovel or uncovering it when clearing out clumps of brush. After scuffing around in the dirt, it was a moment of elation and triumph when one of us found a brass cap. The finder was always rewarded with a "good job" or "nice going" for his discovery, and with the cap exposed we could now read the location stamped on its top. By using a compass we could determine which dams were in that particular section of land and also calculate in which quadrant of the section each dam was located. After documenting the location of a dam, we could approximate its size, and using the height of the spillway could calculate the quantity of water the dam impounded. For two weeks we searched for the caps and dug them out of the ground. We used use the odometer in the pickup or paced off the distances from the caps to the dam in question, and then we had an accurate approximation of each dam's location on the topographic maps. Tom then documented the locations and sizes of the dams.

After two weeks of scouring the land and diligent searching, we had located the 52 dams and calculated their capacity. Tom had documented the information necessary to establish our water rights for the irrigation wells, the windmills, and the water impounded in the dams. It was painstaking work, but well worth the effort to have a legal claim to ownership of the water with the system Pete had perfected. It was the summation of his quest to develop water resources in the dry, desert land. This water documentation was the icing on Pete's cake, and though it was not the final outcome of the ongoing water-rights disputes, it was a necessary first step to secure ownership of this valuable resource.

This project was very valuable and informative for me, and I learned much about the location of important things other than dams on the ranch: the position-ing of the State, Federal, and private property, the locations of ranch assets, and the legal boundaries of pastures and roads. The rules for use by the public were entirely different on all of the state, federal, and private land, and knowledge of the location and legal descriptions of the different parcels of land would be extremely useful in settling any jurisdictional dispute and helpful in investigating crimes on the ranch such as theft, vandalism, trespassing, or poaching. This learning experience of surveying the land was vital in every aspect of ranch management, and especially in planning for further projects on the Corralitos.

10

Bull

The big Brahman bull charged back out of the corrals with fire in his eyes, and was pawing the dirt, flaring his nostrils, shaking his long horns and threatening to disembowel the horses and riders forming an arc out in front of him. The bull was facing off against nine skilled cowboys with ropes in their hands, the riders twirling them menacingly above their heads. But the bull wasn't backing down. This was the most unpredictable, savage, and dangerous bull we had ever encountered. He was a man killer.

The aggressive, ill-tempered bull was one of a herd of 250 cattle we were gathering at the Candler corrals on a hot September day during roundup. The bull was five years old, in sleek condition, and in the prime of his life. He weighed 1,800 pounds and had thick, pointed horns. He could charge in an instant and sprint nearly as fast as a quarter-horse. He had the temperament of a Mexican fighting bull, like the breed of bull used in arenas for bullfighting, and he was just as mean, just as fast and twice as big. He hated people and had little fear of cowboys or their horses. He was in prime breeding condition, and had subdued all other bulls in the pasture to have his pick of the females. He had been released on the ranch for a year and knew every nook and cranny in the pasture, and he hated being corralled. The bull was very much like a feral animal, feeling that all humans were a threat to him. He sensed his status as the dominant bull in the herd, and he had lost his fear of man and would not be intimidated. Howard called him the meanest bull he had ever gathered, and every cowboy agreed.

We were gathering the Mason pasture when the riders first encountered the aggressive bull. The bull at first gathered in with the cows and calves and headed in the right direction to the Candler corrals. But as the riders herded him he would continually stop, turn around and throw his head in the air, shake his formidable horns, and paw the dirt as a warning to the cowboys to keep their distance. Then he would whirl around and continue on following the cows and calves heading toward the corrals. The cowboys could tell by his behavior that the bull was a dangerous troublemaker, and as long as he was heading toward the corrals they did nothing to pressure or aggravate the huge, unpredictable animal. The riders let the bull set his own pace and held back so as not to encourage the bull to turn around, fight the riders, and scatter the herd.

When the herd reached the corrals, the cattle were hot and tired and eagerly streamed into the corrals to drink water and eat the hay we had baited in the mangers. The big bull was in the middle of a hundred cows when he entered the gate, and he started crowding with the cows into the alleyway leading to the main holding pen. Then in a flash the bull realized he was being corralled, and in a fit of rage he spun around in the alleyway and charged back out through the cows and calves to the corral gate, sending frightened cattle scrambling in all directions to get out of the brute's way. The cowboys' attention was glued to the enraged, massive bull facing them seventy-five feet away.

There was only a moment's hesitation in the bull's unexpected burst from the corral gate, and instantly he charged at the closest rider in the semicircle of cowboys surrounding the gate; a dozen frenzied cows and calves stampeded behind the bull in a full sprint, searching for a hole to bust through the arc of cowboys. In a split second the cowboys who had been twirling ropes above their heads broke rank and turned aside and let the furious bull pass by without roping him. They made the right decision. It would have been foolish and dangerous to rope the huge enraged animal charging directly at the riders in tight quarters and in the midst of a mass of fleeing cattle and calves. There was no maneuvering, no ability to make an unobstructed throw, and it would require at least two cowboys—one to rope the bull's back legs and one to rope his head—to fully subdue him. But the cowboys would have only an instant to react to the charging, high-headed bull, followed by a dozen frenzied cows in pursuit. One missed throw of the rope by a cowboy and someone could get killed. We let the bull go, and he crashed through a mesquite thicket near the corrals and hightailed it on a dead run heading north. After quitting the bull, the cowboys galloped back out and to the sides of the stampeding cattle to stop them and turn them around; then they pushed the cows and calves back into the corrals and finished processing the herd. The man-killer bull was on the loose, but we would deal with him in another way, at another time.

We had to gather the dangerous bull and bring him to the headquarters. He was too big a problem to be left out in the pasture. If he threw a fit every time we tried to work with the cattle, we would have a continual problem with the ornery animal that we could not abide. We let the bull cool down for a few days and then tried to lure him in to drink water and eat hay at his favorite watering, the Little Mills Wells corrals. He was a valuable animal in the prime of his breeding life, and we didn't want to injure him by roping him out in the pasture, perhaps having to choke him down and then drag him into a trailer. The cowboys could certainly do it, but it wouldn't be an easy task. Roping him in the expansive, rough pasture would be the last resort. For the next few days, Leonard put out flakes of hay at the corrals and opened the gates into the loading chute. Shortly, the wary bull ventured in to drink at the corrals and began to eat the hay. Leonard threw in more hay each day and tossed it closer to the loading chute. We kept watch on the bull's whereabouts, and in a few days—when he had settled down and was eating in the corrals—we slipped in behind him and closed the gate on the holding pen, trapping him inside with hay and fresh water available. We backed a trailer into the loading chute, opened the trailer gate, and tossed flakes of hay inside. The bull was penned in the corrals with water to drink and hay to eat inside the trailer, and once a day we baited the trailer with fresh hay and then left without disturbing the bull. When he became accustomed to people lurking around the corrals and the trailer containing hay, he cautiously began eating inside the trailer. Within four days the bull had calmed down enough that he would walk into the trailer without fear and eat hay as soon as Leonard baited it. The fourth day Leonard baited hay in the trailer but didn't leave right away; instead, he hid near the trailer and waited until the bull walked up into the trailer and began to eat. In a snap, Leonard jumped from his hiding spot and slammed shut the trailer gate behind the bull. The animal was startled and began ramming and butting the trailer with his horns and trying to escape from the cage he was trapped in, but to no avail. The steel bars in the trailer had finally confined him. We had captured the bull without harm to animal or cowboy, and now it was time to haul him to the headquarters and perform a procedure on him to hopefully quell his aggressive, fighting nature.

We left the bull in the trailer at the headquarters for a few hours while I called the veterinarian and ask him to come out that afternoon and do some work on the bull. In talking with the veterinarian he suggested that the only remedy for such an aggressive animal might be to cut off his horns. This procedure could lessen the bull's savage nature since his horns were his biggest offensive weapon, and without them he might settle down. The procedure certainly would make the animal less dangerous to handle, so we decided to dehorn him. It was really our only choice if we were to keep the animal in our breeding herd. Dehorning the animal wasn't without risks. Dehorning an adult bull with four-inch thick horns would result in considerable stress, blood loss and danger of infection, and we didn't want to lose this valuable animal as a result of any medical procedure. But we thought it a risk worth taking, so our veterinarian would dehorn the bull, and the ranch crew stood ready to assist in the operation.

We set our corral gates to run the bull directly from the trailer into the hydraulic squeeze chute. The bull unloaded with a huff and snort at the cowboys, then swiftly headed down the narrow wooden entry chute, ran directly into the hydraulic squeeze chute and was squeezed tight, securing his head and neutralizing his vicious horns. The brute was no match for the power of hydraulics and there was no way for him to resist the steel's viselike grip. He was completely immobilized. With a surgical saw the veterinarian sawed off both of the bull's horns, leaving four-inch stubs sticking out sideways from his head. There was minimal blood loss, and the veterinarian sterilized the horns and gave the bull injections of vaccine and an antibiotic to prevent infection. Then he bandaged the horn stubs to prevent fly infestation. When we released the bull from the chute, he whirled around and pawed the ground, ready to fight one more time. Then he spun around and fled the corrals in a high-headed trot into the shipping pasture. The menacing horns were no longer a danger, and hopefully the procedure would calm the bull's aggressive nature. But the cowboys knew the bull would be unpredictable as long as he lived, and they kept a watchful, cautious eye on him after he was released. He was still a dangerous animal.

We never gathered or confronted the bull again. One week after we treated and released him, we found him dead beside a drinker in the shipping pasture. He was scarred badly and his left ribs were broken and caved in from a vicious head butt to his side by another bull. The water boy said that on his daily route he had seen the big bull fighting with two other bulls at the drinker earlier in the day. Bullfighting was mean, savage business, and the big bull without his horns was no match for his rivals. Hornless, he was no longer dominant, and fighting against two bulls spelled his doom. The loss of the valuable animal was disheartening. We had worked long hours in stressful circumstances and dangerous conditions to rehabilitate the bull, trying to calm his ill temper and settle him down in the herd, but to no avail. His natural tendency toward aggression was ultimately his death sentence.

II

Troubles

The next five years of my tenure as ranch manager were the most fulfilling years in all my working experience. Both Howard and Lawrence, especially Howard, helped and guided me in making the right decisions for the ranch. Howard's knowledge of all aspects of the cattle business was astounding, and his success as a businessman was unparalleled—things done from the top down with just a phone call. He often came alone to the ranch, and we would spend hours driving the dirt roads, inspecting the cattle, evaluating the pastures, and making plans to increase or decrease the cattle numbers based on the condition of the forage and the state of the cattle market. I learned a great deal from him, especially how to stay calm and focused under adverse conditions, and I relied on him to help me solve the knotty problems that arose daily on the huge cattle ranch. He still loved to tinker with things, and often we would stop at some rickety old barbed-wire gate and repair it with new staves and wire, then stretch the gate properly to ensure it could be opened easily. He was a hands-on uncle and boss, very helpful with even the smallest chores or necessary work It was a pleasure to have him stay at the ranch, to work with him and learn from this successful icon of the beef industry. With Pete's death, he was the man I trusted most in the world.

Lawrence, too, was helpful—and more amiable than he had ever been. But he didn't spend as much time at the ranch as Howard did. He and Bertha would stop by the ranch for a day or two and then head to the horse races in Ruidoso, where they always stabled a couple of horses that were racing at the track. Barbara and I went up several times to enjoy the races with them when work permitted. Lawrence was mellowing with age, and thankfully, his bellicose behavior had subsided. Because of a painful, swelling condition in his legs, he could no longer spend long hours on horseback, but he became content to ride and enjoy his horses, leaving the hard, grueling work to the ranch hands. With inevitable aging, his retreat from the rigors of daily ranch work was a wise decision, and I enjoyed him more at this time than any other time in my life. Lawrence seemed to be more at peace with the world.

Barbara kept the headquarters as neat as a pin, and her record keeping and oversight of the books and payroll were a blessing to the ranching operation. Occasionally when Blanche came along with Howard she and Barbara would spend hours cooking delicious dinners and shopping in old Mesilla for specialty clothing that couldn't be purchased elsewhere. The two women truly loved each other's company and even traveled to Europe together for three weeks. They adored each other and fit together like two peas in a pod.

The alfalfa hay business continued from season to season, but unfortunately the cost of pumping water had increased dramatically. This—along with the unpredictability of the weather during the harvest-time and the increased costs of maintenance and labor to produce the hay—was making the raising of alfalfa hay a progressively less attractive business. So we discussed the possibility of growing other crops and considered other options to farming the 550 acres of irrigated circles.

It was a wonderful time to be managing the ranch, and a learning experience, especially with Howard's oversight. Barbara and I were settled into the reality of ranch management life, the hard work and long hours, the ups and downs of a rural, sometimes isolated existence, and we were thoroughly enjoying the challenge.

At times on the ranch we encountered dangerous people, like the deranged transient who wandered aimlessly into the ranch from the interstate, half naked and delirious, knocking on doors and windows at the headquarters. He immediately became demanding and threatening, and with the ranch hands working in the distant pastures, the women had to defend themselves. Most of the women and their babies cowered and locked themselves in their houses, but Barbara took action. She had a pistol and her 130-pound king Doberman female, Lucky, which she held back on a short leash. The big, snarling dog didn't like the hairy, naked intruder. The dog was very protective of Barbara and would have torn this deranged man to pieces with a simple command from her. Confronting the crazed man with her pistol in one hand and the big dog in the other, she drove the lunatic out of the compound. He vanished into the thick mesquite and was never seen again. Lucky for him that he didn't confront her any further.

Drug dealers and automobile thieves used ranch roads along the interstate to avoid detection by law enforcement, and you had to be vigilant of any person or vehicle on the ranch that you didn't recognize. For no obvious reason, a gang of militant illegal aliens passing through the ranch on foot once did intentional damage to the irrigation wells on their way through, even though we offered to feed them and let them sleep in a warm barn. There were also resident poachers who snared and trapped coyotes and bobcats for their hides—hides stolen from the private and public lands on the ranch—then sold these hides at a good profit. Poachers never bought hunting licenses. They would trap out of season with no bag limits and had no regard for law or common decency. Of all the criminals and crazy people who habituated the ranch, by far the most dangerous were the poachers.

It was legal to trap a few species of animals on the Corralitos, and we always welcomed licensed hunters and trappers during scheduled seasons if they followed the hunting regulations and respected our private property. Many of them were friends. But poachers didn't respect any law enforcement and had no regard for private property and fence lines. They lived in unlit camps or in their cars, sometimes ran their traps with motorcycles, and sought as much refuge as possible from the public eye to conduct their illegal activities. They were feral, living like the prey they captured and killed. At least the poachers were too wise to draw attention by killing or stealing livestock, as that would have provoked a massive state and federal investigation. They were excellent survivalists able to live off of the land, and they made their own rules out in the wilderness. But they were always armed, and no one but trained law-enforcement officers with a warrant should have ever tried to detain or arrest these savage, unpredictable criminals.

The poachers' most dangerous, deadly activity was cutting fence lines around the ranch and along the interstate freeway. They cut the fences so they could get into remote areas without detection, but this sometimes led to deadly car accidents when they cut fence lines that kept our cattle from wandering onto the roads. It wasn't a pleasant evening to be called out at midnight by the state police to an accident scene, to witness the carnage created when a small car traveling at 70 mph collided with a 1,500-pound bull standing in the middle of the freeway. There were always serious injuries if not fatalities, and the fence-cutting poachers were to blame. But it was nearly impossible to catch them in the act of fence cutting, and hard to prosecute them.

But one morning as I was driving north on the county road, a motorcyclist on a dirt bike came out of a dirt road, kicking up dust and traveling fast as he pulled in front of me. We had recently suffered a rash of fence cutting and were pretty sure poachers were responsible. I suspected this guy might be involved with the fence cutting, so I made sure to get a good description of him, the make and color of the motorcycle, and, most important, his license number. I had to react quickly to this guy, because evidence would soon be blown away by the wind. Turning around and heading back to the headquarters, I found Leonard and told him to saddle and trailer his horse and follow me back to the spot where the motorcycle had driven off the dirt road in front of me. When we got to the place, Leonard mounted his horse and followed the motorcycle tracks off road to a spot in the fence line where the poacher had cut all four wires and driven through with his bike. Continuing on horseback, Leonard discovered another fence cut on the perimeter fence line along a county road to the north, the fence line that restrained our cattle and protected the motorists. I headed back to the headquarters and immediately called the New Mexico Game and Fish Department in Las Cruces. I told them what had happened, and that afternoon two officers arrived at the ranch and began their investigation. We led the officers part way by pickup and then walked for a half mile to the two cut fence lines with a backpack loaded with forensic material. There the officers took impressions of tire prints left in the sand by the poacher at each crime scene. I gave them his description, the description of the motorcycle, and the license number.

Within hours the officers had traced the motorcycle to a family living along the Rio Grande River down in the valley. The next day the officers got a warrant to search the property, where they found and impounded the motorcycle whose tire treads matched the tire track impressions they had recovered from the ranch. The family had had previous problems with game and fish violations. The suspect was a 19-year-old guy who had had earlier run-ins with the Game and Fish Department but was never charged with any crime due to lack of evidence. His father, too, had been suspected of violating game laws around the valley. In fact, the whole family seemed to be involved in poaching. The state wanted to prosecute the young man on the felonies of trespassing and destruction of property on state, private, and federal lands. I agreed to testify against him.

The man pleaded not guilty, was released on bail, and went to trial before a jury in four months. The evidence against him was overwhelming, and the jury found him guilty on all charges. Though implicated in previous violations, he had no previous convictions, so he was only sentenced to a year of probation and placed under house arrest during that time. I felt it was a very lenient sentence, considering the gravity of the charges and the dangerous crime of fence-cutting he had committed, but I was content with the verdict because we had sent a message to the criminal element, the poaching community: cutting fences on the Corralitos wouldn't be tolerated and we would respond with criminal prosecution of fence-cutters or trespassers. From that point on, fence cutting occurred only infrequently in the ranch interior, and rarely along the perimeter fences protecting the county roads and interstate freeway. Being able to stop the carnage on the roads and the destruction of private property made it worth all the effort of taking the guy to trial. I was very thankful for the immediate response of the state police, the Game and Fish Department, and the County Sheriff's Office who participated in investigating and prosecuting this horrendous crime.

12

Cowboy work

It was an unusually wet winter with early rain and a late snowstorm that dropped a foot of snow and covered the ground. The earth was saturated with life-giving moisture like I had never seen before, and early in the spring the native weeds began to burst from the sandy soil in abundance. Additional heavy rain soaked the ranch early in the spring and the native vegetation grew rampantly. There was plentiful green feed, a wealth of edible weeds for the cattle to graze in every pasture on the ranch. The verdant desert landscape was luxurious with fodder, and wild flowers blanketed the land with colorful blooms. The cattle gained weight and the cows produced abundant milk for their calves. With all the native vegetation available to graze, the bosses decided it would be a perfect time to import some additional cattle to graze the pastures while the forage was lush. We would import 400 head of young Mexican steers and release them into two pastures, the Mare and the Middle, comprising 21,000 acres.

The steers we imported weighed about 250 pounds each upon arrival. They were shipped from rugged desert pastureland in northern Mexico, pastureland with sparse forage, dotted with thorny cactus, which the Mexican ranchers burned to remove the thorns so the cattle could eat the blackened but edible flesh.

The steers, though needing additional nutrients to thrive, were in excellent condition when they arrived at the ranch. These Mexican steers were called *corrientes*, a word that means "rebel, headstrong survivors." These young animals were very durable, tough crossbreds as rugged as the desert ranches they came from, and they would adapt to the high desert of the Corralitos perfectly. Howard often remarked, "To kill a *corriente*, you had to cut off his head and hide it from him." This was exactly the right kind of steer at the right time to pasture on the Corralitos.

The trucks hauling the steers arrived early in the spring, and we unloaded the steers and ran them through the chute, branding and inspecting each one. We fed the steers alfalfa hay in the corrals to settle them down for two days, and put a couple of cows in with them to help calm them down. The cows would baby-sit with the steers for two weeks when the frisky young cattle were turned out to pasture. We would leave the corral gates open and keep hay in the mangers until the steers were led out by the cows to graze in the two huge pastures rampant with forage.

The steers thrived during the first weeks of their pasturing. They were strong, growing tall and gaining weight, and their hair coats were sleek, glistening in the noonday sun. The steers roamed and investigated every nook and cranny in the large pastures, and could be seen grazing half way up the mile-high Sleeping Lady Hills. There was green feed everywhere in the pastures for the steers, and they were gaining over two pounds a day, a great weight gain for these young cattle. We would graze the steers for six months, and during that time the ranch would receive bountiful monsoon rains that further enhanced the forage. It was the hardiest and most abundant ranch land during that year that I had ever seen, and the steers flourished.

In late September of that year we gathered the steers to ship them to the feed yard, but it was no easy roundup. The steers weighed about 700 pounds each, were robust, full of energy, and didn't want to be disturbed or corralled. They were well acclimated to the terrain, could run almost as fast as a horse, and would defend themselves with their sharp front hooves. The predators left them alone. They spooked easily when we rode through them daily on horseback, and they tended to scatter and hightail out ahead of the riders, looking for an escape route away from any intruding cowboys. The steers were about as feral as a domestic animal could be, and it would take nine cowboys and two days to gather them from the two large pastures.

The first day of the roundup went uneventfully without any bad incidence. We split our cowboys into two crews, half pushing the steers from the northern Mare pasture to the south, and half starting in the south of the pasture and pushing steers north. The two herds were then pushed into the Middle Pasture through a gate at the Big Gap Well, a watering location the ground crew had baited with flakes of hay. About 175 head were rounded up in the Mare pasture and mingled with the additional 225 steers already grazing in the Middle Pasture. The next day would be a more difficult round up in the mountainous, rocky terrain of the Sleeping Lady Hills that split the Middle Pasture in half.

The Middle Pasture was never an easy pasture to gather. There were only two passages or gaps through the mountains to push the cattle, one to the north and one five miles to the south. We unloaded our horses at the western fence line of the Middle Pasture and split the cowboy crew in half; one half would push steers through the northern Big Gap and the other half would herd their cattle through the southern Middle Gap, the only routes through the mountainous terrain. We scoured the western side of the hills, taking our time trying not to spook the flighty steers, prodding and gathering them out of the arroyos and off the aretes high up on the steep, rocky slopes. The steers were very unsettled, running out ahead of the cowboys and splitting apart from the herd. The riders didn't want the cattle to run; it caused weight loss and stress on them, but the steers were not content with the cowboys moving them in the pasture and were doing their best to evade the riders. We had to keep a cowboy riding along the ridgeline to keep the hightailing steers from escaping back into the hills, but it was difficult for a rider on the ridgeline to keep pace with the steers because of the wash-outs and arroyos, and at times the rocky, steep terrain slowed the ridgeline rider to a walk, giving the steers an opportunity to get out ahead of the cowboys, turn and flee back up into the arroyos and escape.

We had pushed the steers ten miles and were only two miles from the headquarters corrals when a dozen steers suddenly broke away from the herd and ran at full speed to the west and entered a wide arroyo with sheer rock faces on both sides. I was riding alone on the flank near the middle of the herd when the steers bolted away 200 yards in front of me, and there was no way I could I could get in front of the cattle to turn them around before they hightailed it up along the north side of the arroyo. I was in a gallop behind the steers, but it was useless to chase the bunch from behind and it would only speed up their breakaway, so I quit from behind the steers and began climbing along the south side of the arroyo in an effort to get around the cattle so I could turn them back. The arroyo ended at a sheer rock face midway up the side of the hills, and below that rock face was a small saddle, the only spot in the arroyo where the steers could cross over and escape to the north. There would be no other riders in front them to turn them around, and if they got away over the top of the arroyo at that saddle they could run for miles and it would require an additional round up and another day to regather the large pasture.

I was on the south side of the arroyo and the steers on the north, and we were both in trot on the hard slippery hillsides trying to reach the saddle of the arroyo. If the bunch got there first they would escape over the top. At times I had to slow to a walk and give the horse his head so he could safely navigate through the deep holes and rough spots, and I still had half a mile to climb before I reached the saddle halfway up the hills. My horse was scrambling to keep his footing in the treacherous ravine, but slowly, after fifteen minutes wending our way up through the brush, boulders, and deep holes, I reached the top of the saddle only seconds ahead of the steers. I spun my horse around and faced the bunch still climbing up the grainy slope, trying to pass over the saddle to freedom. The animals were determined to escape past me in that narrow spot, and I was just as determined not to let them. It was a face-to-face confrontation on top of the arroyo, and I was outnumbered twelve to one. It was a show-down.

The saddle was only thirty feet long, and the steers were now below me, spreading out across the length of it and still inching up the gravelly slope toward me, resolutely trying to find a spot along the saddle where they could bolt past me. I unlatched my rope from my saddle-horn and pounded the coils on my chaps, whooping and hollering at the steers, reining my horse from side to side, lunging back and forth along the top of the arroyo, making a racket, creating as much disturbance as possible, the horse and I becoming as large and threatening as we could. If one of the steers broke over the top, the rest would follow in seconds, bolting over the saddle and hightailing it down the side of the arroyo.

I continued dancing my horse back and forth across the top of the saddle, reining him right and left with just a touch of the spurs. His ears were laid back, with his eyes glued on the steers. The horse understood the standoff we were in and was doing his best to turn these critters around. Then suddenly, when the steers were four feet from the top of the saddle, they stopped in their tracks and decided to climb no further; they turned around and scampered back downhill into the arroyo. The runaway was finished, and much to my relief the cattle were now hightailing it back toward the corrals with me close behind in pursuit. I saw Pacheco on the north face of the arroyo. He had come to help, but was now holding tight to let the cattle pass by him in the bottom of the arroyo. Then he fell in behind the bunch, and together we drove them two miles to the headquarters and corralled them. We would let the entire herd settle down in the corrals overnight with fresh hay and water, and the next morning the trucks would arrive to load them and ship them to the feed yard in California.

That evening at the back bar, Art—a veteran cowboy—told me he had seen my entire tussle with the headstrong steers in the saddle, and said I had done a great job in turning back the runaway steers. Art was riding the ridgeline and had climbed to the top of the hills to get a better vantage point and scan the pasture for any straggling steers. He was fifty feet directly over me at the top of the rock face, and staring down at me in the saddle as I contended with the steers. There was no way for him to descend the sheer rock face and help me turn the steers back. He never made a sound, knowing it might distract me or spook the steers and send them bolting over the saddle, and I never knew he was there. I wasn't the best cowboy, didn't have the horse sense or hours in the saddle of Pete, Howard, or Lawrence, and didn't have the years of hands on experience of most of the cowboys I rode with, and my skills with a rope were only average, but I loved gathering cattle on horseback. It was a precious part of my life. Cowboys gave few compliments, and when Art related his story I was thrilled and beaming with satisfaction of a gathering well done, and I thanked him.

13

Farewell

Bertha Daley died of cancer on January 6, 1989, just a few days after Lawrence and Bertha's 50th wedding anniversary. The funeral was in San Diego and the reception at historic Rancho Jamul. Hundreds of people attended the services and the reception that followed at the old ranch house. Her son, my cousin George, displayed all the oil paintings she had done of the ranches, the blue sage mountains, landscapes of lush pastures, barns, and old early homesteader dwellings. Her paintings of the scenic areas along the California coastline were thrilling. It was remarkable artwork—strong, true, and timeless, like the artist. The whole family was heartbroken, of course, and in tears. Lawrence was grieved and quiet. We had lost a matriarch, a keeper of the peace and a provider and protector of the ones she loved. Her ashes were spread along a creek that flowed through a pasture in the scenic valley around the ranch house. Bertha was my second mother, and I was saddened at her loss, but happy and content that she was in a better place and no longer suffering from the ravages of her disease. Aunt Bertha could never be replaced and will never be forgotten.

Lawrence remarried within a year of Bertha's death. He was in his late seventies and his health was failing. The many years of hard, backbreaking work he did as a young man were now taking a toll on his body. It was a circulation problem; his legs would swell and become very painful, and he suffered greatly as a result. His new wife, Bobbie, had worked many years for Lawrence and Bertha as a cook and assistant to Bertha. She was a hard, dedicated worker, preparing delicious meals in the cookhouses of both the Bernardo and Jamul ranches. It wasn't easy work preparing and serving three meals a day for a crew of fifteen men, then having to clean up the kitchen and start cooking again for the next day. It was tedious, never-ending work, fourteen hours a day and seven days a week. Of all of the ranch workers, she was always the first to rise in the morning and the last to go to bed at night. Lawrence was fortunate to have her because she was a good person and would take care of him in his last years. She had four children by a previous marriage, and Lawrence would be loving and generous to them.

In 1990, a prolonged period of drought on the ranch was affecting ranch finances. The cattle were showing the effects of little green feed and dwindling native pasture. The hay market was depressed and the cost of pumping water was very high. It had not been a good year in the ranching or farming operations, and the cost of maintaining the ranch had escalated. In an effort to save money, we quit the large-scale haying operation and leased out several hundred acres of irrigated land to another farmer to grow lettuce, which was very successful, but the income from the leases still was far short of what we needed to operate the ranch. We had to do some drastic cost-cutting of ranch expenditures, laying off some employees and reducing capital expenditures to maintain the ranch equipment and purchase any new equipment, especially the pickups used to run the hundred miles of water lines and pull the stock trailers. It was a bitter pill to swallow, and I wasn't happy or content with any decision to cut off funds to maintain what I thought to be vital equipment to operate the ranch. Lawrence and I had some heated conversations about the reduction of operating expenses. He wasn't really wrong—his economic position was certainly justifiable, and if I were in his shoes I undoubtedly would have made the same decisions. Nonetheless, I was still determined to stand my ground, and I refused to accept a dramatic reduction of operating capital, knowing the increased workload and decreased standard of living it would impose on all of us living and working on the ranch. I knew that if I crossed Lawrence and didn't accept and obey his orders, I'd be fired. But I also knew I couldn't continue to manage the ranch successfully without his continued financial backing and support of my management decisions during this very stressful time. So my tenure as ranch manager would soon come to an end.

Lawrence and Howard arrived at the ranch early one morning in mid-December, 1990, and terminated me. Howard was sullen and sad, but he abided by Lawrence's decision, and I respected him for that and loved him. Lawrence wasn't happy having to terminate me either, but he and I had both drawn lines in the sand about budget cuts; he did what he felt he must and I did what I felt I must. I respected his decision and still loved him, too. Barbara and I, after fourteen years, would leave the Corralitos.

My tenure on the Corralitos Ranch was the most satisfying and thrilling experience of my life. It was a combination of business and family, filled with hard work, with delightful but also painful, difficult decisions: business decisions that sometimes necessarily—but only for the moment—overshadowed family unity. We all cherished the lives that we had lived and the loved ones who made it possible. The men were dedicated to producing beef and crops that sustained the family, and the women were devoted to working hard, to soothing the difficult, tedious job of ranching, and to inspire harmony among the families. The children were required to obey and assist in the daily chores given to them that would enrich their lives and fit them to become productive adults. If you lost the respect of the family, you lost everything. Barbara and I relished the rural life on the Corralitos Ranch. It was fulfilling for both of us, with new adventures each day—an enriching, wonderful time in our lives that is captured forever in many memories of dedication, perseverance, and love.